GOD WITHOUT FEAR

An experience of exploration into the nature of God

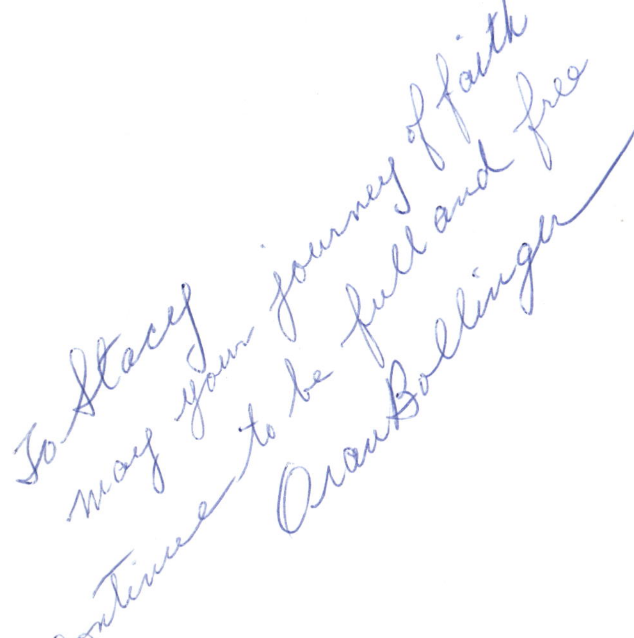

A theology in a nutshell

ORAN BOLLINGER

Dedicated
to
the men and women
who are serving to protect
world peace
and
who are searching for
eternal meanings to life

Acknowledgments

Thanks to W.H. "Bill" Gilbert for encouragement and support; to the Rev. Richard Brown for ideas and proofreading; to the Rev. James Trotter, retired Episcopal priest with a Master's degree in English, for theological and grammatical proofreading; to my wife for her patience and editing; to my son, David, for computerizing the manuscript; to Larry Prieto for his illustrations; to Paul Thompson for page designs; to "Laura," "Gayle" and all the people who have asked pertinent questions about God throughout fifty years of my ministries and chaplaincy.

Thanks to Tyndale House for permission to use passages from The living bible; copyrighted, rights reserved.

Thanks also to Ann Christensen at Word Design of Modesto for the cover design.

Orchid Publishers, Inc.
P.O. Box 1699
Turlock, California 95381

TABLE OF CONTENTS

THESIS

GOD WITHOUT FEAR

"Perfect love casteth out fear"
I John 4:18

There are two basic propositions for this writing. First, God is pure love; He is compelled to be loving toward whomever is before Him. Second, God is and has been actively revealing Himself to mankind throughout history. A study of religions show many identical thoughts about God, indicating His desire that we open our minds to understand His will.

This is not to ignore the various paths mankind has taken in searching after God. Rather, we should be eager to search different paths to find how they reveal elements of the Eternal God.

Because our purpose is identification of basic underlying principles of God, we will strive to lay aside cultural influences, religious rituals, humanized concepts and scientific perceptions which seem to conflict with general religious beliefs.

Since love and fear are emotions, and both are experiences, it is logical to call this exploration **"EXPERIENTIALISM."**

Jesus began His calling of disciples by simply inviting them to experience Him. His call to Peter was: "Come and see" (John 1:39). The disciples experienced Him for three years: they experienced the healing of the sick; feeding the hungry; making the lame to walk and the blind to see. They experienced the dead restored to life; they witnessed Jesus upon the waters and calmed as He stilled the storm. They enthused over the power of His spirit when He taught them the loving truths of God. They experienced the horror of His trial and the crucifixion, and rejoiced when they saw His resurrection.

Intellectual pursuits are commendable; scientific researches are important to the understanding of our lives and of the universe. These studies, however, can also present disturbances. Religion, education and science need integration.

v

Hearing testimonies about God from other people can open doors, but only through experiences can one declare with Paul. "I know in whom I have believed" (II Tim. 1:12).

Religious experiences can be rejected by humanistic scientists, psychiatrists, psychologists, ones who glory only in themselves and other skeptics who claim that they are mere self-delusions, projections of desires, hallucinations, dreams, personified fantasies, folk-lores and superstitions, but they only voice an opinion. Those experiences cannot be proven wrong.

Human nature is such that it seeks approval and a sense of belonging. Even enemies come together to get support against a mutual danger.

Religion cannot exist without support. It must be shared with others and gain adherents or it dies.

Mahavira, founder of Jainism in the 6th century B.C., said: "All must attain one's own salvation, no rituals nor priests can do it. Each person must find salvation within himself." He continued, "Man! Thou art thine own friend. Why wishest thou for a friend beyond thyself?" Then comes a paradox: for thirty-five years he had crowds about him as he taught persons to be isolated!

Jainism thrived because these people not only sat and listened, they became evangelists broadcasting its teachings.

The logic, or thesis, of this book is:

"GOD IS LOVE" (John 4:8).

LOVE IS AN EMOTION.   EMOTIONS ARE EXPERIENCES.

"PERFECT LOVE CASTS OUT FEAR" (1 John 4:18).

"KNOW THE TRUTH AND THE TRUTH SHALL SET YOU FREE" (John 8:32).

"IF THE SON SHALL SET YOU FREE, YOU SHALL BE FREE" (John 8:38).   LOVE FREES YOU FROM FEAR.

EXPERIENCE THE LOVE OF GOD WITHOUT FEAR.

INTRODUCTION

Experiencing God through group discussions is not a new concept. Searching for ultimate realities is a historical quest every human being makes. It is a philosophical exercise in the sense that there can be no "scientific" data to prove the quest--nor are there any data to deny the quest's discoveries.

Group discussions enhance discoveries because of "togetherness." On the other hand, group discussions can fail if any individual within that group expresses strong rejection to the group experience. Because of a book's limited space, a congenial group has been selected so that discussions may be involved with sincere questions. "Any fool can ask questions which even the wisest sage can't answer," was said many, many years ago. These discussions will be based on: "No sincere question is so small that it is not important."

Because "the group" indicated herein is a composite of many groups through more than fifty years of discussions, names will be used fictitiously. No name is intended to identify a specific person, living or dead.

THE GROUP:

Laura; A student of psychology with strong fundamental beliefs in Christianity, and having a life-style which reaches out to help other people.

David; A college student intrigued with scientific data which deals with origins of the universe and mankind. He is a musician, a mathematician and a computer expert.

Jesse; a practical wage-earner seeking to know how God can be influential in his life.

Jennifer; Jesse's girl-friend. She is excited about living her life and relating to God.

Gayle; a school teacher who recently had an intimate life-changing experience of seeing God in her life: eager to learn more about the reality of God.

You; these questions can be your questions because you may be involved with the discussion. Our aim will be communicating with you.

     <u>Others</u>; sometimes other persons will enter discussion with new questions and will then be identified.

     Chapters will be formulated as discussion sessions with a theme question as the topic. There will be repetitions when the questions lead to a basic discussion in other chapters, but this is the way of discussion groups.

     Each member will be encouraged to ask "stupid" questions, or to make "stupid" remarks, recognizing that insights often arise from the simplest inquiry. Much significant input will be drawn from old Hindu writings since that is some of the earliest written material of mankind's search for meaning.

     Archeology's discoveries of significant facts regarding the practices and possible beliefs of prehistoric humans will be considered. Myths, superstitions, folklore, social behaviors and needs all lend light on the origins of religious beliefs. Discussions will strive to be inclusive rather than dogmatic; we do not intend to declare: "This is the only truth."

     As suggested above, a spiritual awakening is an individual matter. It could be heightened by group "arousements," but what was received from that group emotion or experience must be accepted as an individual's experience or it has no personal value.

     In order to have spiritual answers to the questions of life, you must internalize relationships to God. This book is written to challenge you to think and to take on the adventure of going "where no man has gone before" (Theme of "Star Trek," a science-fiction series on T.V.). An obvious point is whether anyone has gone there before or whether anyone ever will journey out there, **WHAT IS REAL IS REAL!**

     This is just as true with God as it is with the distant and unknown phenomena of the universe.

     Be not deceived--no one knows the mind of God. But, God knows our minds and our needs. This seems to be certain: inasmuch as all societies through all of time have had some religious ideas, God must have been busy revealing Himself from the time Man first was able to think. Therefore, our endeavor will not be to discuss differences religions have devised for their concepts of God, but what the religions had in

viii

common in their understandings of God. Do not hold the bias that all religions but your's are false.

In order to get a picture of how mankind developed the concept of God, we will consider some very early religious beliefs.

In his book, RELIGION OF THE WORLD (From Primitive Times To The 20th Century), Berry states that religion had its birth in the fears of early man, so his life, which was inherently dangerous and uncontrollable, created a fear-related view of nature.

Primitive man had very little control over his surroundings, therefore his survival depended on nature to provide him with favorable conditions. Only the most basic forms of shelter were available, and they were regularly threatened by wind, rain, storms and draughts. These earliest humans were most likely hunters/gatherers. Their sources of food constantly were at risk from those elements.

Before mankind had even formulated the idea of a god, there was a glimmer of religion in the manner uncontrollable forces were revered. These incomprehensible powers were such a significant part of the daily existence that primitive Man was compelled to relate to them in much the same way as he relates to any other living creature. Without means of averting these dangers, he probably cried out to them begging them to cease, or flailed his arms about in order to disperse them. If successful, these acts could have become a sort of a ritual, or a practice, regarding the specific force being pacified.

This personification of natural forces grew to be the first nature-gods. The ancients noticed that winds blew upon them and seemed like the breath of a great Being. Rain fell from the skies and appeared to be the tears of that Being. Whenever the ground trembled and quaked it was as if the Being was walking upon it.

There is a saying in the military that expresses the manner in which primitive man may have first conceived of a god: "Everyone is religious in foxholes." Or, put another way, "There are no atheists in front-line foxholes." Dangers generate "prayers" for help.

Imagine yourself living in the ignorance of the dawning of humanity. You are walking along and stub

your toe on a stone. You immediately stop to make a
tribute to that stone. You recognize that stone to
contain a spirit, a god. It may be good or bad, but
your need is to give it some type of recognition so
it will not jump up and make you stub your toe again
when next you pass this way.

This same type of projection is to be found in
the fairy-tale of the hen who felt an acorn fall on
her head. Something happened! There had to be some
kind of explanation. The acorn came from above. The
sky is above. Logic: the acorn was part of the sky,
therefore, the sky was falling!

It is interesting to observe that with all the
noise she made while she went screaming that the sky
was falling, no other hen accepted her testimony.

In the same manner, religious experiences often
go unrecognized by other people. People who receive
a mystical experience are often judged to be insane,
mystics, charlatans or fools.

Strangely, personal mystical episodes are called "mountain-top experiences" but are so unexplainable that the light of another day may make us doubt
our own experience. We are unable to force them to
happen again, and we can not transmit those mystical
elations to another person. We can only bear a witness to what we experienced. Sharing may encourage
other people to open their hearts to God's abundant
love, however.

Mystical, ecstatic, heart-felt or transcendent
experiences can come upon persons who are in a set-
ting of meditation and elation. Being open to spiritual awareness allows the supernatural to become
known to us.

Ancient Greeks sought oracles for answers. The
oracles were approached by mediums, priests and the
priestesses who demonstrated a communication ability
with deities. They utilized numerous techniques to
get messages from the gods: natural gasses in caves,
incantations, altar fires, herbal drugs, drawing en-
trails from chickens or animals, casting lots, reading palms and the shape of head. Some were probably
just plain fakes.

Buddha sat for seven years under a tree having
a starvation diet so that he could subdue his body
and elevate his spirit into Nirvana. He formulated
x

an elaborate system of "steps" which souls must attain in order to escape reincarnations.

The Mayans used intoxicating herbs in order to induce visions and have ecstatic feelings. Some of the other Indians found different ways to escape the bonds of the body and experience euphoria: smoking a "peace-pipe" seems to have come from the practice of using tobacco as a method of mind-altering; certain cacti were found to produce dreams and fantasies.

While not all mind-altering practices may have been searches for God, it is certain that many cultures have been obsessed with searching for some way to liberate the spirit from limitations of the body.

The "whirling dervishes" of India thought they were gaining liberation of their spirits by spinning so long that they became dizzy and went into comas.

India is full of soul-fulfilling persons today. The United States and Europe are being inundated by "Swamis" who teach Hindu mysticism as the way toward human happiness. Some gurus teach personal achievements, but they can not direct their followers up to celestial realms because they do not believe in the existence of a Universal Reality. Parrinder stated in his book: "The Jains do not admit of a creator or a god" (246). "Salvation" is defined as the gaining of freedom from endless transmigrations.

Hinduism's fundamental teachings are based on a do-it-yourself belief. It has gained strong support in Europe and in America because it offers peace and meditations such as is seldom found in Christianity today.

On the other hand, Biblical prophets were taken by surprise. God chose those to whom He would give His messages. We can almost hear the response, "Who? Me?!" Some of the prophets had only one appearance, or task, while others had life-long relationships.

Note that Paul, the New Testament's missionary-evangelist, was on his way to Damascus to put an end to those who believed in Jesus, but he was stricken by the spirit of Jesus and changed to become the one to carry Christianity throughout the Gentile world.

He could not reject the vision, but he was certainly surprised!

The following discussions will endeavor to show some basic precepts about the nature of God, taking into account some of the revelations given to other religious beliefs. Great social and religious truth can be found in ancient writings.

We will use the Bible extensively because it is the documentation of God's redemptive love. Jehovah (YHWH, or "Yahweh"), is the Judeo-Christian God and His intentions for mankind are displayed throughout the Scriptures. While attending seminary, my professor of religion wanted us to recognize that myths, allegories, folklore and other fanciful stories only attested to the accuracy of this ancient collection of religious writings. There's no other sacred writing which contains such information.

Persons in the Old Testament were actualities. They loved; they fought wars; they argued; they became sick; they rejected Jehovah; they became slaves of other nations; they had dreams of a Promised Land which they would some day inherit; they returned to the Lord and He led them in paths of righteousness; they cheated and lied--they were God's chosen people to be His witness. But they were not perfect angels!

Because the Bible speaks of real people, you'll find yourself in it. Our discussions will show how they progressed in understanding God, but it took an extraordinary event to fulfill Man's destiny: it was necessary for Jesus Christ to come into the world in order to provide Man with a way back to God.

These discussions cannot "prove" a thing; their searchings, however, may help another traveler find his own experiences with the God of love, and in the finding of that know that he has all the proof that can be known.

WHAT IS "IN THE BEGINNING"?

**"In the beginning God created the heavens
and the earth."
Genesis 1:1**

The ideas of "beginning" and "eternity" oppose each other. This discussion will be involved with semantics--the meanings of words. It will need definitions in order to limit our discussion toward any specific goal. As I've said before, we do not have an absolute answer, but we shall endeavor to arrive at some logical understanding.

Greek philosophers, modern journalists, writers and modern police investigations and research scientists insist that we have the who, what, when, where and how answers to arrive at a logical solution. You have asked the "what" question; it will also include the "when" consideration.

Laura, "Doesn't it also include the 'who' question?"

Of course, but for the discussion tonight let's limit ourselves to the action of beginning.

"Is that what Stephen Hawkings calls a 'singularity'?"

Yes, and he also calls a "Black Hole" a "singularity." What do you think he means by that term?

"Here is what the dictionary states," Jennifer answered. "It means something which is unique, only happening once. It could refer to a person who is a leader or outstanding. I guess that would indicate that Stephen Hawkings is a singularity!"

Yes, and many other persons in history would be in that category. Even you might be a singularity.

The "Big Bang" theory dates the origin of this universe to that instant of time when absolute nothingness exploded into everything. Hawkings says it was not a cause-and-effect happening, but the singularity of chance.

That's not a good term, either. For something to have been caused would necessitate the existence of a causation. A builder has to have raw materials

from which to build. The idea might exist, but ideas
themselves are not buildings. Ideas need materials
with which to become realities.

I'm purposely allowing you to become uneasy--a
bit restless to discuss the beginning. Maybe if we
re-phrased that question so instead of asking, "What
is the beginning?" we should ask, "What was begun at
the beginning?"

"That's easy," Jesse offers. "Haven't we just
read that the beginning meant the creation of heaven
and earth?"

That's true, but that is not exactly what I am
trying to get you to think about. Did the beginning
make a difference? If so, and I assume that you all
agree that it did, what kind of differences could we
be talking about? Was it a start of something from
nothing? Can there be an even greater significance?

Gayle: "You said something about semantics. Is
this what you are driving at? If there was nothing
before the beginning, we will have to define 'beginning.' Are you suggesting that there was something
before the beginning? I am getting a funny feeling
that we may be thinking of TIME, not THINGS."

In our comprehension of reality, "yes." God's
understanding of reality, it seems to me, might have
the answer, "no."

Confusing? Not at all. It only seems a confusion because we are in the habit of thinking in the
stream of time. Eternity exists outside the stream
of time.

Gayle's observation about something <u>before time</u>
implies movement before the beginning of time. That
does not correlate with eternity because there is no
movement to eternity. Eternity is that which is now
past, that which is at this moment and that which is
to be--all rolled together.

The Bible says that God is Alpha and Omega, the
beginning and the end. It does not say that God was
the Alpha, neither does it say that God will become
the Omega. It simply states that God exists as both
at the same time.

We asked, the beginning and the end of what? It
could not be that eternity had a beginning, nor that
eternity has an end. It's meaning could be that the
moment "time" began God was there, and that when all
14

"time" comes to an end God will already be in there in the ending.

The book of Hebrews writes of Jesus, "the same yesterday, today, and forever" (Hebrews 13:8).

One way to describe eternity is to see it being always at the point of this moment of time. Eternity doesn't have a "was" (past) tense; neither is there a "will-be" (future) tense. Eternity always stays in "now." From the time of God's statement: "I am that I am" (Exodus 3:14), to the declaration He makes in the book of Revelations: "I am Alpha and Omega," God uses the present tense.

"In the beginning" doesn't relate to eternity, but to the beginning of the passage of time. It is interesting to observe that the Bible outlines six periods of time to the creation process:

<u>FIRST DAY</u>. This is the period of darkness into which light was begun. Genesis 1:1,2, the beginning of the Bible, gives a picture of the universe before "the beginning." Let me illustrate that day on the blackboard, realizing that such a beginning would be impossible to realistically portray!

This board has nothing   WATER   WATER
on it: it is darkness.
Think of it as having   DARKNESS
no limits: it is void
and without shape.   WITHOUT FORM
Think of this blank
space as totally,   VOID
eternally dark.   WATER   WATER

The first thing to be added to that darkness is light. God called it "day," but it did not change, it just stayed "light." All that darkness was composed of water, as the second day will indicate.

The first day isn't ended yet; the light spread out through the darkness. Although God called the light "day" and the darkness "night," it was not a changing of periods as today--no earth yet for such changes.

"The beginning" had started.

<u>SECOND DAY</u>. The second period, or "day," isn't easy to comprehend. Since Bible was set in the comprehension of the people who wrote it, it is strange to our understanding today. Thinking about the universe as being composed of water, there had to be

a place for earth, so they thought that God formed
the "firmament" to hold the waters away from earth.
That opened a space for creation.

Here is a drawing
of what it may have
been thought to be:
Note that God did not
have to be very big
to cover this universe.
He could sit in his
"heaven" just above
the firmament and see
the whole world.

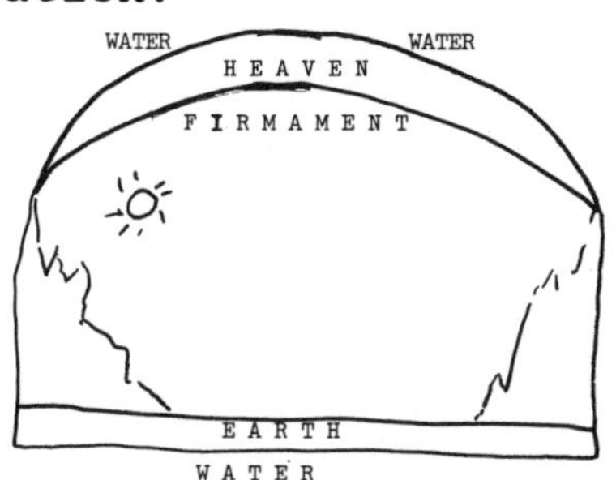

THIRD DAY. With a bubble of air in place, the
dry land and the oceans could be formed. The change
in the picture for this day would only be the growth
of herbs, grasses and trees, which were necessary in
the next phase.

FOURTH DAY. Now came the completion of the sky
and the changing of days and nights. The sun, moon
and stars were identified.

Our picture
takes on more
detail. There
is no explana-
tion of what
happened to the
sun and moon as
they changed

positions. I suppose they might have thought there
was a tunnel under the earth where the sun, moon and
stars made a return journey.

FIFTH DAY. With the sun to give warmth and the
herbs and grasses for food, it was time for animals,
fish and birds to appear.
Earth was still a
bubble, but there
was room for all
sorts of living
things. God
looked upon His
creation and
found it to be

good. That goodness was not perfection. God still
had not brought forth a creature of His own image.
16

<u>SIXTH DAY</u>. All of nature was ready. "And God created man." Into the Garden of Eden came Adam and Eve.

Just for fun, here is another fanciful picture for you. The bubble is still there; water is still around everything; only

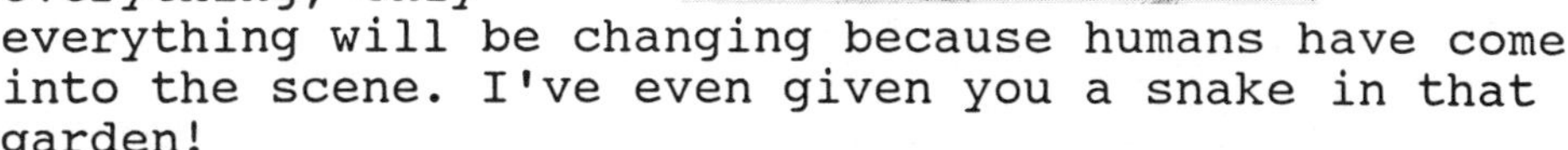

everything will be changing because humans have come into the scene. I've even given you a snake in that garden!

<u>SEVENTH DAY</u>. "And God rested from his labors." There has been no physical creating since that day. The implication of this day is that God is now resting and doing nothing.

I have never read a scientific description for the beginning which did not exactly follow the outline give in the Bible.

Isn't it amazing to realize that when the Bible was written such an exact chronology could have been conceived in a time when nothing about the universe was known?

There were no scientists then; no cosmological theories; the world was considered flat, perhaps no bigger than Ireland; the "firmament" was thought to be not much higher than a four-story building. The Tower of Babel was intended to reach into the nearby firmament (Gen. 11:9).

"How long did the beginning take?" Jesse asked. "I have heard heated arguments about that. Someone told me that the periods for creation you have been talking about had the same number of hours as today. They say that all carbon datings of deposits of coal and oil, petrified forests and frozen mammoths, fossils, artifacts of prehistoric humanoids, evidences of earthquakes, seismic shifts, movements of earth's plates which heaved ancient ocean bottoms into present-day mountains and archeological finds of ancient civilizations were instantly created by God in those first six days. That would be only one hundred and forty-four hours for creation. I think that is what is called, 'fiat creation'. Other people tell me of

an evolutionary creation which took many billions of
years."

    We will never know for sure. Frankly, I am not
bothered with how long God took to form the universe
we now have. I believe in the logic of God; it might
be the universe evolved under His direction. It May
be that God created the world instantly. I believe
in miracles.

    I attended church which believed the universe
had been created in six days with twenty-four hours
each. My inquisitive mind was never satisfied when I
asked what God did during the seventh day. After a
twenty-four hour rest, what did God do? What "day"
are we in now? Where did God go? Isn't He active in
our world or in our personal affairs today?

    That church believed in what is called "predes-
tination." I was told that God designed and planned
for everything in the world through all of time, and
that when He set things in motion everything had to
proceed just as He had destined them to do. Then, I
was informed, God left and had no more activity with
anything. He lives in eternal rest. I was told that
we can not make a choice because our lives have been
determined from the very beginning. It was not to
be confused with "fate," but was the will of God.

    I eagerly perused through John Calvin's volumes
which systematized predestination. It is likely that
I began to rebel when I read his comment saying that
God willed little infants to be born in sin and that
if they died in infancy they would go directly into
hell. One of his illustrations was that there were
babies in hell no bigger than "the span of my hand."
He explained that the horror of infants in hell was
the horrible background against which the glories of
heaven could be compared!

    What you think about "the beginning" can make a
difference in how you envision God. If you can get a
glimmering of the difference between eternity and
temporal, the time relationship, you have a start in
your own theology. That word, you know, comes from
the Latin word for God, "theos," and the one meaning
for science, or to study about, "ology." Theology is
the study of God. Merely practicing rites and creeds
is not theology. The excitement of theology comes
through experiencing the unfolding vistas of God.
18

IS THERE A GOD?
"The fool hath said in his heart, there is no God."
Psalms 14:1 and 53:1

Your question, David, is basic to any study of the universe, of humanity or of God.

We must start out by recognizing that there are no absolute scientific proofs for God. Neither are there any proofs against God.

There is no absolute proof of how the universe came into existence.

There is no absolute documentation about how human beings, homo sapiens, came into being.

We will be discussing some theories and beliefs as we go along. What I am encouraging you to do is to keep your minds open so that you can explore the amazing vistas of both scientific discoveries and religious thoughts and experiences.

Before we get involved in our discussions, let me take a moment to state that I will be using the generic word, "Man," to designate all people. It appears to me that God must have had an understanding of our present conflict with that word when He is recorded in Genesis, Chapter 1, verse 26 (shortened to: Gen.1:26) as saying, "Let us make man in our own image, after our likeness, and let them have dominion..." Verse 27, however, reveals that Moses (commonly accepted as the writer of Genesis) slightly missed what God said, he wrote: "So God created man in His own image, in the image of God created He him." It took a lot of effort to carve that stone.

You all know we can't put words into the mouth of God, but let us create a little fantasy.

Suppose that when Moses wrote the above statement God looked at it with eyes into the distant future and exclaimed: "No, no, Moses. You didn't understand what I said. I created both males and females to be equals. I used the word 'them.' You wrote 'him.' That could produce a misunderstanding."

"Gosh. I only tried to be accurate and write what You said," Moses replied defensively.

God's love reached out to soothe Moses. "I understand. However, we can't let coming generations think that I am only concerned with men. Hmmm, let Me think a bit. Well, you can't erase the stone; I guess you had better add a clause to what you wrote so that it will be clear to everyone that I created them to be equal: the woman and the man are to be equal. Just add that I created males and females."

So Moses chiseled God's instruction onto the stone: "In the image of God created He him; male and female created He them" (Genesis 1:27).

Using the complete word "humans" or "humanity" all the time is bothersome. I don't want to seem to be using "sexist" language so I am asking you to grant me the "poetic license" to utilize the generic meaning of "man." To designate when I am being all-inclusive, I will capitalize "Man." I will do the same in reference to God.

Uncapitalized "man" will indicate males. Uncapitalized "god" will indicate the idols, trinkets, charms, figurines and deified personified thoughts and objects Man has created.

Ah, yes. I heard that whisper, Jesse. You think by capitalizing "Man" it could be thought to equate that word with God. That can not be, can it? My purpose for going to such length with this is to make it clear that I am just using a simple technique in order to make it easier to refer to all persons.

But that has gotten us away from our question: "Is there a God?"

David, you said you asked this question because in school you were assigned to make reports about such books as, "The Death of God" and "God Is Dead." You might be surprised to find that these modern books are not modern thought. Go back to what we read in Psalms about the fool thinking in his heart that there is no God. That would not have been written were there no people in those days declaring that there wasn't any God.

Now, let us discuss how Man developed a conception of God. We will have to look at primitive Man and find how they might have lived.

Do you know how and when our concept of the universe developed? The discussion about creation included the idea of earth being flat--and small.
20

Consider that the entire Bible was written when scientists were believing that same concept.

Let's take time now to consider some changing ideas about the universe.

First, the Biblical "flat universe." That world could be calculated as being from the Mediterranean Ocean to the Tigris-Euphrates rivers; from the mountains north of Babylon to the deserts of Arabia.

Many local tribes did not have even that large an image of the world. Their religions had to conform to the size of their universe; therefore, their religious concepts were very limited. They couldn't have had a comprehensive vision of a universal God.

Hindu religions had a larger view but was quite vague, The Chinese, Babylonians and Egyptians had developed astronomical knowledge showing an expanded universe, but this also was vague.

Columbus wanted sail directly West in order to get to India, but the scholars of that day declared that he would drop over the edge of the ocean if he sailed "beyond the gates of Hercules." That was in 1492. Modern science of the day still proclaimed a flat earth.

Then came the telescope, gravity and Columbus. The world became known to be round. Earth became the center of the universe.

Ptolemy drew the new system to look like this:

Each unit of the heavens had its own circuit. Space was still confined within the solid "firmament." The moons of Mars and the rings of Saturn were discovered and added to those circuits.

New astronomical discoveries made the sun seem to be the center of the planetary system, and the center of the universe.

Copernicus, another astronomer, formulated this picture:

The "firmament" was still there. Outer stars were still in separate circuits under the solid sky.

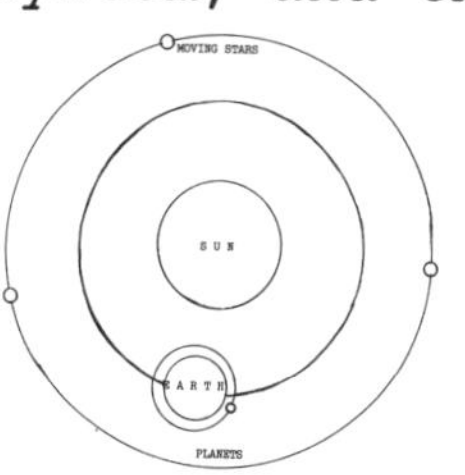

God still lived in heaven, which was still pictured as being just above that firmament.

There was strong religious and scientific opposition to each new discovery. Some people continued to believe the earth was flat.

Today, the "expanding universe" is so complex and mind-boggling that there is no ultimate theory.

Einstein tried to make reason out of the vastness of space and declared that everything was relative, and that space was curved upon itself like a gigantic ball, somewhat like Copernicus' encircling firmament. He did not conjecture as to what existed beyond that ball.

I am told that modern scientific logic proposes a "fourth dimension" into which the expanding universe is growing. Many astronomers accept Einstein's theory of the curvature of space. The universe is conceived to be like a giant balloon with everything located on the surface and rushing away from everything else as it expands.

Berry's book RELIGION OF THE WORLD (From Primitive Times to the 20th Century), says that religion had its birth in the fears of early man. David, my son, used Berry's statements to document a college paper about the life of primitive Man, a life which was intensely dangerous and uncontrollable.

He wrote that Man's survival depended on nature to give him favorable conditions. Only basic shelter was available.

Winds, rains and lightnings were always dangerous. Man was a hunter and a gatherer whose source of food was endangered by these natural forces. A lack of food and scarcity of water made those primitives migrate to distant lands to find suitable habitats.

Berry's book and David's paper probably detail how God had to reveal Himself before mankind was far enough advanced to picture a loving God.

Before there was any idea of personifying God, the forces of nature required attention. The uncontrollable forces of nature were so frightening that ways to try to please the forces and to escape those awesome terrifying powers had to be developed.

They probably developed dances and rituals, and built special places where the terrible forces could be appeased. As the simple practices evolved, they would naturally lead to a deification and personification of natural objects and phenomena. They experienced rain falling from the sky, and probably saw the gods to be weeping. Winds blew like human breath and made them think it came from the gods. They fell when they stubbed their toes upon a rock--the rock must have had a spirit which jumped up and cause the accident. The flower was beautiful because a happy spirit was living in it. The brooks sang happy songs when cascading over rocks. The sun was a god giving warmth and life. The moon and stars became endowed with religious symbolisms.

Worship of nature-gods is called "Pantheism." The making of images and idols to be "gods" which contained features of animals, birds, other living things and objects is called, "Anthropomorphism."

The fairy tale of the hen who thought the sky was falling when an acorn fell upon her head illustrates how easily mystical interpretations can be made about ordinary happenings. Note that as she ran around the barnyard screaming that the sky was falling, no other chicken listened to her story.

That hen's attempt to convey to the other chickens what she thought was true is similar why so much of religion is not accepted. Mystical experiences are hard to explain to others who are skeptical. They also become strange even to us when remembered from the perspective of another day.

Laura: "That is exactly what happened to me. Last summer at church camp I felt so close to God that I was sure He held me in His arms. Sadly, that feeling gradually faded away. I can only remember what a wonderful feeling it was. I've tried to bring back the same feeling, but I can't make it happen."

"And that is the reason I have been searching," Gayle added. "About a year ago I had a strange experience with God that changed my outlook completely about everything. Where once I took things as just a matter of course, considering religion as just something relating to a church, now I can feel the workings of God in almost everything in my life and in the things about me."

Your experiences are not unique. History shows many persons with mystical experiences. The Catholic Church has looked upon some of the magnificent mani-

festations as being from God, and has called these
people "saints." Today's society might label such
people as being deluded or suffering from hallucinations and confine them to mental hospitals.
Many people desiring mystical experiences are drawn
to Pentecostal churches where manifestations of
being filled with The Holy Spirit are accepted.
Let us put our observations into an outline:
1. We have discussed that some type of Divine
    consciousness has always been present in
    Man. This has been seen in archeological
    digs and in pre-historic drawings in caves
    and on various stone walls and cliffs.
2. Experiences of people through the ages
    verify the workings of God in human life.
    These experiences are dismissed by skep-
    tics as being fantasies, dreams, emotion-
    alisms and psychological disturbances.
3. Many scientists have looked at the meaning
    of life, the mysteries of creation, and at
    purposes in living and have concluded that
    God must exist.
4. Greek philosophers were constantly talking
    of human-like gods. Their ideas showed the
    religious interest of their thoughts.
5. Widely separated religions by space and
    time show an amazing similarity and agree-
    ment regarding the basic beliefs about
    human relationships and the basic nature
    of God. This indicates communications from
    God rather than from human inter-actions.
6. Science used to teach that all things must
    come from something. Modern science theor-
    izes that creation had its origin out of
    nothingness--the Quantum Theory. A theory
    was needed to explain how the "Big Bang"
    could eventuate from nothingness and cause
    the creation of this physical universe.
7. Logic points to the necessity for there to
    be a God. Accepting God to be real brings
    all of the above quandaries into focus and
    provides an explanation of the universe.
8. Logical conclusion:

<u>THERE IS A GOD!</u>

WHEN WAS GOD BORN?

"I am Alpha and Omega, the beginning and the end, saith the Lord, which is, which was, and which is to come, the Almighty."
Rev. 1:8

Your question at the last session, Jennifer, is a very natural one. We exist in the motion of time. We are born. We live. We die. We plant seeds which die, but live reborn into plants and flowers.

Earth is constantly presenting living cycles where we find not only nature changing, but the very earth undulating with the formation and decline of plains, mountains and continents. Our language is cluttered with "thens," "nows," and "whens." We form tenses: past, present and future in order to know how to use proper English and to communicate better.

We study ancient religious thinkers and find a birth day for Confucius, Buddha, Mohammed, Moses and Jesus. Why should we not ask when God was born?

Reaching for answers about eternity can be very frustrating. The answer may be very simple truth if we are willing to take a leap of faith.

If you analyze your question, Jennifer, you may see that it includes "Who were God's parents?" Logic would cause us realize that a birth would require a medium through which the birth could occur.

Laura protests, "But, nothing in the Bible says anything about God's parents!"

David: "That's right. To ask about the parents of God brings us to another quandary: 'Who were the parents of the parents of God?' Going back into the origin of origins is never ending, a useless philosophical exercise. That's the same as asking where the material for the 'Big Bang' came from."

Good reasoning, David. That's how logic can be used to make us think. Blind faith usually makes it unnecessary to ask questions or to give answers, but such a faith is often not logical. Is it not better to believe in a God who is logical?

Jennifer's question is logical. Paradoxes will
show two concepts which may appear to differ, but a
comprehensive picture can reveal them to be sides of
the same truth. A diamond has facets facing different ways, but all of them are pointing inward toward
the heart of the diamond. Religions may differ, but
all point to God, by whatever name He may be called.

Jesse, impatiently: "You're not letting us get
to the question Jennifer asked. I am aware that our
Bible starts out with the statement that in the beginning God created the heaven and the earth (Gen.
1:1). But even the thought of creation contains the
necessity that God already existed, it doesn't tell
us when or how God was born."

How would you answer that question, Jesse?

"I don't have the slightest idea about how to
answer it! Are you just going along with Jennifer to
show that there is no answer?"

Not at all. I just said that I think we should
see all things about God as being logical. The problem is to get our minds ready to accept that practical, mystical logic of God.

Here is an illustration which can be made meaningless even as I tell it, but it may provide a way
to describe our relationship to God. Let me suggest
that God is like a computer's disc full of data. A
scanner applied to the disc can read the information
only at the instant it is contacting the disc. That
scanner always reads the disc in the "now" position.
The disc, on the other hand, is always in possession
of all the data: that which is past, that which will
be in the future of the scanner, and that now being
read by the scanner. If the disc were intelligent,
it would be aware of what it contained, it would be
existing in the "now" of the past, as well as existing in the "now" of the future, and existing in the
"now" which is this instant.

You protest: "But the disc would need to have
a beginning. Someone programmed all that data into
the disc. There was a time when the disc had nothing
on it--when the disc was "ignorant" and timeless. It
had to be made; it had to be born; it had to be programmed; it had to learn; it had to grow."

Aren't you glad you came to the discussion? You
are a logical thinker. You do not just accept what

other people tell you without seeing if it makes any
sense to you. I think God is pleased with that kind
of reasoning. On the other hand, I think God is not
pleased when we just close our thoughts and refuse
to look into the meaning of things.

Let's get back to what you said about the disc.
You have picked up the point I was trying to make in
the beginning: there is no illustration that can be
analyzed apart from the purpose of the illustration
and still make sense in the entire story. Illustrations have to be accepted for the point they are designed to cover, not as a total item to be analyzed.
The disc was used as an illustration that showed the
difference between "time" and "eternity."

Look at the illustration Jesus used as He called the fishermen to be His disciples (Matt. 4:19).
He said that if they would follow Him they would be
fishers of men. That is a good, logical invitation
to become an evangelist and to bring the message of
salvation to those who are lost.

Now remember, I am purposely taking Jesus' allegory apart to demonstrate that the entire meaning
of the illustration can be lost. Taking the idea of
being fishers, think about the fish. The fish were
perfectly happy living their fishy lives. The fisherman comes along and catches them--they are thrown
into panic and terror when they are netted. They'll
die when they are removed from their environment.
Has the fisherman helped the fish?

We have already discussed how we live within a
moving stream of time. This very instant is "now."
We cannot move backward in order to live yesterday
over again, nor can we advance one instant ahead.

Take the other view of time: the disc doesn't
have any movement of itself; it is "eternal." And,
although it is stationary, it would be aware at each
instant of everything upon it. The disc would have
no need to go back to yesterday because all "yester-
days" are it's present realities.

The second thing to consider is that God, like
the disc, exists timelessly. I cannot really grasp
what it means to say that eternity stretches forever
into the past and forever into the future, but I can
believe and accept that that is the meaning of eternity.

Someone asked Stephen Hawking, the author of A SHORT HISTORY OF TIME, if God existed before the Big Bang singularity. Stephen Hawking is considered by Carl Sagan to possess the greatest mind within mathematics and astrophysics since Albert Einstein. Inasmuch as his book is on the origin of the universe, it was natural for him to be asked about God.

Hawkings answered that his research dealt with the singularity of the Big Bang and afterwards. He said that what might have been before that was only philosophical fantasy; thus, not fit for scientific considerations.

At a recent meeting of the Catholic Cardinals, the Pope was asked a similar question about how far into the past Catholic scientists would be permitted to explore. The Pope answered that it was the duty of all scientists to investigate everything, including looking back in time to the Big Bang.

"However," he stated, "God can not be discovered by scientific research; God can only be found by faith."

God can not be inherited. God may be intimately experienced by an individual, making that experience seem similar to the act of being born. Such an experience is not the birth of God, however.

Every religion I have studied has revealed some kind of a creation story. They all show some Power working to produce that which was created. To have done the creating, God had to exist before the act of creation.

Elementary? Obviously, but the question of when God was born is just that rudimentary.

Who can put this discussion together and arrive at a logical answer as to when God was born? I have suggested that there is an answer.

Gayle: "I think I understand what you are getting at. Since God existed before the beginning, or the Big Bang of about four billion years ago, and He will continue to exist; and if the eternal tomorrow is the same as the eternal yesterday, are we forced to conclude: God exists without being 'born'? Maybe we are confused with a terminology about the motion of time; maybe there is a need to have another word for the timelessness of God. Comprehension of ideas depends on the clarity of the definition."

28

Jennifer: "Does that mean God is something like this ring which has no beginning or ending? When I look at a ring I have to start someplace."

Not exactly, Jennifer, but it's a good analogy. Ancient religious thinkers of India had plotted all the changing seasons, the movement of stars and wondered at the meaning of existence. They thought the universe and eternity were linked together, similar to a circle of sausages. Every life of a universe was like an individual sausage: it had a beginning, and it had a definite end. That ending was the death of another universe. Death of a universe was not the end of time, however, there were other universes out there waiting to be born--the birthing of the next sausage in the unbroken circle of eternity.

Universes were not reincarnated, but newly born worlds which had to create their own destinies.

Even gods died with the death of a universe. A reluctance is shown in the Hindu sacred writings to declare that Krishna (Vishnu), Supreme Consciousness of the universe, would die when a universe died. In fact, the writings indicate that Krishna existed as The Personality which dwelt apart from rebirths.

David: "I guess I shouldn't be bringing doubt-things up, but I've read that many people think the word 'God' is just a kind of super-ego made from the thoughts of many human beings. These people seem to think that when, or if, humanity dies, that superego will die out also. In their thinking, God came into being when humans sent out imaginative thoughts and created a god."

Would it make you happy if you could believe that this is all God is?

"Not really," David replied. "It's just that so many people are claiming that God is only a psychological phenomenon. It is like the proclamation of the Russians that there is nothing to religion, that a religion is just a ruse to pacify people. Russia could never have considered the question of when God was born."

What we have been trying to do in this discussion is to paint definitions of something our minds will intellectually accept, but which we may not actually comprehend. You are not alone when you have trouble thinking about eternity or infinity.

The Psalmist wrote: "A thousand years in Thy sight are but as yesterday" (Psalms 90:4).

Don't think of religion as the only place where you come upon terms that cannot be comprehended. If you consider Stephen Hawkings' "Black Hole" as being infinitely compact and containing unlimited energy, I'd have to ask if you comprehended that? The terms have to be relative. It is not scientific to employ ambiguous definitions. Just think about it: to be so infinitely compact would require a density and a smallness which could neither be seen nor analyzed. It would make the point of a needle be "infinitely large" in comparison.

Infinity has no beginning--nor can it have any ending. Stephen Hawkings, however, describes Black Holes as having beginnings and ultimate endings.

Consider the concept of "space." An "expanding universe" has been the center of scientific conjecture for hundreds of years, but no one has answered the question of where space came from.

Einstein thought he had found an answer when he proposed the curvature of space. He thought that if you shot an arrow into the sky with enough force it would eventually hit you in the back of the head because it would be on a straight spacial line, which would actually be the circle of curvature of space. No, he did not say how long you would have to stand there in order to be hit!

A problem with Einstein's theory is that it has no answer to what lies outside that circular globe. We are faced with what amounts to a dogmatic religious reply: "That is a question which is not allowed to be ask!"

Want still another puzzle to carry home? When Astronomers look at the stars they find them moving away from us at a tremendous speed. No matter which direction they may look, the stars racing away from us. That is the expanding universe.

The Big Bang theory proposes that this "singularity" caused all matter to be hurled out into all the universe in different directions and with equal amounts of force. Wouldn't it seem that some of the matter which was hurled along a similar path to ours would not be receding at the same rate as that which is on the other side of the of the Big Bang?

Here is a bit of humor:if everything is receding, an extrapolation of that concept would retrace the paths of stars and find them all right back here at our solar system. Scientists seem to gather data which confirm Ptolemy or Copernicus who thought the earth or the sun was the center of the universe!

These scientists are also not satisfying the question about the nothingness of space into which that Big Bang's matter is rushing--some call it the fourth dimension. (We'll be mentioning that "Fourth Dimension" later, even naming it!)

Just recently a new "monkey wrench" broke upon the Big Bang theory, which declares that all matter was dispersed evenly. Astrophysicists have located a giant wall of stars which they measure at about a million light-years high and many millions of light-years long. That wall is so far away its light must have traveled through space for billions of years to reach us. It may be necessary to reconsider dating the origin of the universe. That is not all. A mere two months later that electronic sensor detected another star-wall even farther away, and even larger.

"Let me add something to that," Jesse said. "The January 3, 1991, issue of THE DENVER POST wrote that a critical element of the Big Bang theory (the even distribution of matter) is being questioned by some of its former advocates. A new Infrared Astronomical Satellite shows the universe is full of such super-structures and super-voids.

"It said that these new discoveries present new facts which disturb astrophysicists who have assumed cold invisible matter is the prime attractive force of the universe, based on the Big-Bang theory. "These "super-walls" are too huge and far away to have been formed since the Big Bang. Now there's a need for a new theory to explain the beginning and expansion of the universe."

If distant star-walls are really many billions of light-years away, doesn't this make the origin of the universe have to be pushed back a few trillions of years? That may be a slight exaggeration but it high-lights just how uncertain our present knowledge of the universe really is.

<u>Scientists do not always have the final truths.</u>

These mind-boggling astronomical findings only illustrate that eternity cannot be measured, nor can God be correlated with material things.

There are be many, many exciting discoveries to be found in this amazing universe.

Discoveries so far have shown logical progression. Could such an orderly universe be chance--or was it designed?

Revelations quotes God: "I am the Alpha and the Omega--the beginning and the end" (Rev.1:8).

John declares: "All things were made by Him" (John 1:3).

God was not "born," but exists as the Everlasting Personality of the universe.

Last week was the annual meeting for the church I attend. The meeting was April 18-20, 1991. That date is significant because the worship message was presented by Dr. Marjorie Suchocki, the professor of theology at Claremont School of Theology, Claremont, California. She went back to the beginning of time as she used John 1:1 to showed how the Bible states the "Word" to be God's creative actions. That same verse states the Word was with God; but it said more than that: it proclaims that the Word <u>was</u> God.

Many times we hear this expression, "Your word is my command." We also hear, "My word is law!"

There are many places in the world where something spoken creates action. Dr. Suchacki spoke of how the passage declared Jesus was the Word of God; the Word was the activity of God; and Jesus Christ, the active Word, was God.

A future discussion will elaborate on the person of Jesus.

WHERE DID GOD COME FROM?

"Behold, the heaven and the heaven of heavens is the
LORD'S thy God, the earth also, with all that there-
in is."
Deuteronomy 10:14

This question comes from people who think that
God is in a particular place. They reason that were
God in Chicago, He would have had to come from some-
place, but where?

There's also the thought that some great cosmic
civilization may have visited earth sometime in the
past and brought God with them. Or, "God" might be
just a term carried over from that visit, referring
to those great celestial voyagers.

Archaeologists are intrigued by ancient paintings in caves and upon rock walls which seem to have
religious connotations. Many paintings depict what
could be extra-terrestrials with space suits.

"Doesn't everything come from somewhere?" Jennifer asked.

I think that to be true of material things, but
how do we answer the problem of non-material things?

When the Mayans built the huge worship pyramids
they pondered the mystery of the origin of Man, and
super-human spirits and powers. By experiencing the
great power of the sun they concluded that God must
be the sun. They did not seem to question where the
sun came from because they always saw it in the sky.
The Mayans were involved with questions about of the
origin of Man, however.

They had no theory of the origin of the universe, or where the gods came from. Just as the stars
are always there, so the gods have always existed.

But Man is different. Man was born. Man lives.
Man dies. Man had to come from somewhere, and, having come from somewhere, it was obvious that the essence of an individual had to return to somewhere at
death. Their beliefs were much like those expressed
in the Bible: Man came from the gods; Man returned
to the gods.

The Mayans believed that humanity spewed out of the mouth of a great snake-god when it came out from its hole in the ground; therefore, they reasoned, a soul went back into the snake-god, wherever that god might be.

Mayans were avid astronomers. It could be that they were looking for a heavenly residence for their gods, but no evidence points out that this had been their intent. Astronomy provided the data for mathematics which carried over to religion. They seemed content in the belief that the gods lived somewhere, but did not localize where that might be. There has been no evidence found to indicate they had much of an idea of a heaven.

Religions which believe God dwells somewhere up in heaven, not actually upon earth, must formulate a way for their gods, or god's messengers, to descend and ascend in order to communicate with mankind.

The early Israelites believed God was a tribal guardian. The story of "Jacob's ladder" illustrates just how limited they thought God was.

Open your Bibles and read the story of Esau and Jacob in the 25th chapter of Genesis. That passage will prepare you for understanding why Jacob thought he had to flee.

The Israelites held to the religious obligation of the passing on of the family's name and wealth to the first-born son. This story tells that there was a change in the womb when Jacob was ready to be born first. The process got reversed and Esau became the first-born son, robbing Jacob of the inheritance.

The story is used to justify Jacob's actions as he recovered the blessings belonging the eldest son.

Esau was the rugged hunter. Jacob stayed home to help out with household chores and to work in the fields. Note the difference of family relationship. Isaac loved to eat meat, so he favored Esau. Jacob, being home and assisting with the chores, was favored by his mother.

Only a father could give the blessing of inheritance. A family's wealth and happiness were sealed upon whomever carried God's blessing.

Rebekah enabled Jacob's finagling with Isaac: Jacob received the family blessing. That made Jacob to be the ancestor of Jesus, not Esau. Jacob became
34

no longer a mere household fixture, but the ancestor
of a great nation and a forefather of Jesus.

Jesse, how would you feel if you were compelled
to live your life in a servant role? Do you honor
Jacob and his mother for manipulating his father into giving Jacob the blessing?

"I think I would have been much like Jacob," he
responded. "If Esau wasn't concerned enough to value
what he had, Jacob did a logical thing as he refused
to give Esau food until he gave away his birthright
for a bowl of stew."

Now, turn to the 27th chapter and read the con-
consequences of that bargaining. Jacob had received
Isaac's blessings--by accepting his mother's cunning
help. Jacob wasn't a physical match to Esau. Rebekah
urged him to escape before Esau came home and found
out what had happened.

Assuming the meal to have been late afternoon,
how far could Jacob flee before night came upon him?

Jesse: "A good runner can make a mile in about
four minutes, but he could not keep it up. If he ran
ten miles per hour and kept running for three hours,
he could possibly be thirty miles from home. I think
Jacob could have done that because he was terrified
and had added adrenaline to keep going."

You have recognized that Jacob succeeded in robbing his brother and fooling Isaac, but even worse,
he had stolen God's blessing. Yes, Jacob certainly
was running in terror. It was a terrible sin to rob
God of His blessing.

Back to our question. When Jacob slept, he had
a vision of a ladder reaching from earth into heaven
with angels ascending and descending on it. Angels
indicated that God was present.

WHERE HAD GOD COME FROM? He was supposed to be
back there where Isaac lived!

Jennifer, "May I tell a little joke?"

Serious thought can often benefit from a little
humor. Tell us your joke if you believe it will en-
lighten our discussion.

"It's about a boy who asked his mother where he
came from. His mother was not prepared to tell him
the facts of life. She told him to wait for his father to come home and ask him. The boy impatiently
waited for his father's return. Jumping upon him as

soon as he came through the door, he asked his father where he had come from. The father had read that if children ask questions such as this, they are old enough for an answer.

"Not yet ready for such an intimate revelation, the father nevertheless took the child onto his lap, took a deep breath told him all the facts of having a baby. He didn't want to miss a thing! He finished by asking his son if that answered his question.

"The boy answered: 'No, father, that's not what I wanted to know. Jimmy said that he came from New York. What I wanted to know was if I came from New York or if I might be from somew other city.'"

Yes, that does fit into our discussion. We sometimes ask a simple question to learn of God, but we get very detailed answers which we can't understand.

Let's get back to Jacob. We've discovered that God was thought to be in localized areas, not everywhere. At the end of the day Jacob probably believed that he had traveled too far to be in the presence of God anymore. His amazed question was: "How had God been able to get way out here?" (Gen.28:16-22).

The story of Jacob's vision gives us new understandings about the presence of God.

Jacob was not elated to find out that God was in that place. He was afraid. He built an altar as a warning to travelers that they had better be careful because God was even in this place.

The next day he went to the home of his uncle, believing he was entering the sphere of another god.

The second thought of how God might be here may be a strange thought for you, but not for people who build images, idols and shrines to local deities. A logical question would be to ask about where a local god came from. The question has the hidden implication that if you think God to be so localized, your concept of God is too small.

Swami Prabhupada translated ancient Hindu texts in his book, SRIMAD BHAGAVATAM. He wrote that there are thirty three million (33,000,000) gods in India. These are not eternal deities, but they have been "discovered" by people who thought these gods posessed some kind of mystical power. There are numerous groups in the United States, as well as in European countries, who are following Hindu "gurus."

The enticement of Krishna Consciousness is that when you achieve the full awareness of Krishna, you will also become as a god. A question could now be asked of you: as a god, where did you come from?

Many things in this world defy answers. Can the giant figures on the plains of South America be explained? How can the long smooth roadway resembling a landing strip for airplanes--or space-ships--which was built on a South American mesa be explained? Or how can the huge trident drawn upon the cliff of the eastern coast of Brazil which points to the airstrip be explained? Those figures are too gigantic to be conceived by earth-bound builders; they appear to be shapes only when viewed from thousands of feet above them. Where did they come from? How can we explain their purpose?

Other archeological finds, pictures and images excite all sorts of conjectures. There is no answer to these mysteries. Did ancient astronauts use them as signals? Did they depict feats of conquest? Are they attempts to communicate with people of earth? A primitive tribe in Africa performs an annual worship ceremony with rituals which are directed to a certain star in the heavens, as if space travelers landed in that region and established a ceremony by which they could be remembered. Maybe these people are supposed to be ready when those celestial "gods" return? The ceremony does take on the appearance of religion.

Keep in mind that early mankind considered the earth to be very limited and flat with a solid bowl resting over it dividing the waters above the firmament from the waters below the earth. It wasn't too difficult to imagine having visits from beings above that firmament.

Where did God come from? The concept of timelessness allows us to understand the existence of a God without Him having to come from anywhere.

"I know you are basing your conclusions on experience and logic," David said. "However, sciences may differ with conclusions which haven't a factual base. I've thought a great deal about your illustration of the little red hen. It seems to me she was broadcasting false warnings. Her experience had her think the sky was falling, but she was mistaken.

"Mystical religious experiences are liable to be mistaken interpretations also," David continued.

There are many things which can't be documented by scientific data. Greek philosophy enjoyed asking questions like: "What color is a brick in the dark? Grant that bricks are red in the light of day. How would a scientist go about to prove and document the color in the dark of midnight? Will he use a match so he can see? Will he shine a flashlight to light up the brick? Will he make chips of the brick so he can examine them in the light of day? No data gathered by such scientific techniques would answer the philosophical question. The scientist would change the question and produce an answer, but the philosophic question would not have been answered.

The same problem confronts scientists involved with proving emotion, documenting ghosts, explaining the control of gravity or attempting to bottle a ray of light.

The philosophers asked, "What would happen if an irresistible force met an immovable object?" You might propose an answer to that by pointing out that a force may be an ex-ray or a cosmic ray which goes through "irresistible" objects without hesitation.

Ridiculous illustrations? Philosophizing maybe is not scientific, but it is honored as being on the fore-front of exploratory thinking. Religion is in the classification of philosophy. It should be recognized as having the same non-documentable truth as is granted to the rest of philosophy.

Einstein said that time is relative, having no absolute measurement. Eternity is also relative in that it has no absolute measurement in time. It may be illustrated by understanding how "stop" is related to "go."

We have to keep in mind that we are not trying to "prove" anything. Religion can only be "proven" by faith. Faith will only become individually factual by the experience of accepting the eternal love and presence of God.

Now to your question, David. I have been waiting for the right data to be present so we can agree together. First, we had to arrive at an understanding that science and religion have an essential base for unity. God permeates both science and religion.

WHERE IS GOD?

"Thou art there, O Lord."
Psalms 139:8

This is the question David asked during last week's session. Whoever thinks about God will come to this question eventually, and there will be many answers. Look at this jumble of letters I have put on the blackboard:

G O D I S N O W H E R E

Ancient languages often contained no spaces between words. Readers just had to know how to divide the writing into meaningful words. Reading, as you can see, was a special work for only a few wise men. Can you make sense of those letters on the board?

Just for fun, let us make some attempts at trying to make words out of those letters.

GO DI SNOW HERE. That sounds a little like it might be German, but it doesn't make any sense. Can we translate it to say, "Go to snow here"? That is not too good, is it?

It may be slang: "God, I snow here." Or, "God, I snore here!" That statement is silly.

Put it into our southern dialect: **"God, I's now here!"** That sounds like the shout astronauts could have made when they stepped out onto the moon. And, it could be the cry of disgust made by the prodigal son made when he found himself eating with the pigs.

"I have a problem with that foolishness," protests Laura. "That is not getting at the question of where God is. It seems to me those letters could be divided to say, **'GOD IS NOW HERE'.**"

Excellent, Laura, that would make sense. "God is here" is certainly a Biblical thought. From the Old Testament we get many passages referring to the presence of God, like when He walked in the cool of the evening in the Garden of Eden, (Gen 3:8). It is the same in the New Testament when Jesus promises, "Lo, I am with you always" (Matt. 28:20).

Remember the amazement Jacob had when he cried
out: "God is here!" He thought God was "there." Is
God here, or is God there? Theologians have struggled with that question for centuries because it has
so many possible interpretations. Let us be satisfied with just the straight-forward thought that God
is here. God is where you are.

Jesse, "But what would happen if I divided the
letters to read, **'GOD IS NO WHERE'**? We would return
to the thought that if God is no where, we would be
saying there is no God."

Or could there some other meaning, Jesse? I'm
glad you saw that phrase. Can you see another meaning? How about the rest of you? Can someone clarify
what that phrase might mean for Jessse?

Gayle: "maybe I can help Jesse a little. I see
both sentences having meaning as they relate to each
other. Isn't it possible that when I say, "this instant God is here," I can also believe that He isn't
here? That is, I do not think that the total of God
can ever be in one place. I am trying to grasp the
immensity of the universality of God. It is something like the air I breathe. When I take a breath of
air it is with me, but just because the air is in me
does not mean that it is all of the air."

"But, I have been taught that God is sitting on
a magnificent throne up in heaven," protested Jennifer in a confused voice. "I have been told that God
has need of millions of angels to carry His messages
so that we can know what He wants us to do. We return messages to tell God what we need. With all of
the work He has to do, He's much too busy to listen
to every human being all the time."

David breaks in: "Then there's the thought that
God started the universe and set the whole thing in
motion. Everything that happens was planned by God
from the very beginning. After He started all these
things, God rested. He is sitting on that heavenly
throne, letting the world act out His scheme without
changing it or intervening.

"This is a similar thought as comes up in Greek
philosophy about the three spinsters who weave cloth
for individual lives and snipping it off as fate may
happen to choose. There is no way to change fate. No
prayer to help us. There is nothing God will now do
40

about the pattern of our lives. This thought denies
that God is 'here,' because He is always 'there.'"

Yes, David, that is what my church taught when
I was a teenager. The concept of fate is similar to
the religious term, "predestination." Christianity
seems to be the only religion of the world which has
the concept of predestination. True, the Hindu idea
of reincarnation seals the new birth of a soul into
the pattern earned in a previous life, but that concept of the soul rising or degenerating according to
how the life is lived does not correlate to a rigid
predestination which cannot be changed.

Hinduism is solidly based in fatalism. "It is
the will of the gods" can be heard for the explanation of everything in life and nature. Hinduism can
not promote the idea of freedom of choice.

Fate and fatalism are deterministic patterns.

The Chinese also have the concept of re-births
that are stages set according to learning and experiences of the previous life. Their soul grows as it
lives, so each succeeding life grows wiser than the
present one. Poor people and criminals are merely on
the first round of existences. That is the explanation they give as to why certain people attain such
wisdom: they are in their eleventh and last round of
existences. These "rounds" are not the same as the
Hindu "reincarnations" because the Chinese think of
a continual progression of the individual. There is
no regression into lower existences.

"If there are so many different concepts about
where God is, what are we to believe?" Laura asked.
"I like to believe that God is here to hear me pray.
I know the world is in quite a mess, but I prefer to
think that God is active in our affairs. I think of
that time Jesus looked over Jerusalem and wept over
it because the people would not hear Him. It caused
me to think about tears in the eyes of God."

Thank you, Laura. "Tears in the eyes of God."
That is a deep, deep thought. We will have to meditate about that for a while. There are many theological propositions within that little phrase, but we
will have to hold that discussion for a later date.

Let's go back to Gayle's explanation. How much
of her thought makes sense to you--that God can be
present with each of us, and also be with every one

else around the world, even present every moment of all our lives? No one knows an absolute answer, but I think that the logical and the consistent love of God would have Him present with us always because He cares for us.

We have to accept that most of the things written in the Bible are written from the comprehension limits of the people of that particular time. Just because we tell children about Santa Claus, a tooth fairy, Easter bunnies, ghosts, goblins and the other characters of childhood does not guarantee that they exist, nor does it negate the reality of spiritual, social and moral truths these characters represent.

Paul wrote in one of his letters, "When I was a child, I spoke as a child, I understood as a child, I thought as a child: but when I became a man, I put away childish things" (I Corinthians 13:11).

How many of you have experienced having to change your ideas as you grew older? All of you have. You girls played with dolls and listened to them as they talked with you. That was real to you then, and it was more than just play-acting, wasn't it? Why not talk with those dolls the same way today?

"Why pick on just us girls? My brother had his toys he talked to. He used to scare me with dragons other and monsters. Let me tell you, his dragons or monsters were real enough to me then, and they must have been just as real to my brother," Jennifer protested.

That was sort of stereotyping girls and boys of the day. That is the manner in which society thinks it should train a child. Girls are sweet and gentle, so they are encouraged to play with dolls. Boys are rough, tough and ferocious, so they are given "manly toys" to play with. I have also seen girls fighting with their brothers for the chance to play with the soldiers and monsters.

What I am trying to point out is that as we become older we put away childish notions and take on that which is more meaningful to us. The same thing happens in our understandings about God. A child is taught that God is a "Father." Where would a child look, then, to get an understanding of God? Fathers give a child the first image of God. What responses can we give to help children understand God?

Really, this may be frightening. It is understandable that children fear God when they see their own fathers as frightening. Children hearing their mothers and fathers quarreling often have nightmares about a God being quarrelsome and unlovely to them.

What has all this got to do with our discussion question! I let you continue this way because there were concerns being expressed about different images of God, but they were directly related to our topic. Both religion and science are constantly changing so we change our viewpoints in order to answer the new findings about ourselves and the universe. Mankind, like you, had to start out as infants in its understanding of God. So many things about God have been written that even if you were a speed-reader, you'd spend many hundreds of years just to read the books already written about God. You would have to learn many hundreds of languages where religious writings have been made.

When you finish all the present books, several more books will have been written as you read! This makes it impossible to ever read the last book. But what if you could read the additional books? There would be tons upon tons of magazines, papers and all kinds of writings continuing to pile up for you.

The author of Ecclesiastes has this to say: "Of making many books there is no end; and much study is a weariness of the flesh" (Ecclesiastes 12:12). It may be possible that he had tried to read everything in print!

He ends this book: "Let us hear the conclusion of the whole matter: Fear God, and keep His commandments: for this is the whole duty of man" (12:13).

Again I say to you, no one can be certain what the beginning was, nor when it was.

We can become very confused if we read dogmatic declarations which declare opposite views. Listening to the many different voices telling about God or becoming involved with cults can destroy faith.

I believe that God is logical, meaning that we should approach the mysteries of God with a logical openness. Have this understanding also, God's logic is not be the logic of Man. The most logical thing we can do is to have an open mind so we can grow in our understanding of God's mysteries. The exciting

thing is that there will always be new and amazing
vistas to explore.

"Does that mean we are to accept all the stuff
science brings up to prove evolution and the theory
that chance is the answer to everything?" David was
exploring conflicts. "I am trying to understand how
matter can come from nothing. I think it was a Greek
philosopher by the name of Pythagoras who proposed
the idea that through all eternity an infinite mass
of atoms had been falling in parallel lines. By mere
chance something happened and sent one atom off its
course. That began a chain-reaction from which the
universe was formed. Where did the atoms from?"

You have given us an excellent illustration of
pure chance, David. "Chance" doesn't answer origins.

Let's take some time to visualize a few ancient
beliefs about our world. There is evolutionary unfolding of knowledge in the Hebrew-Christian cosmology. At least, I have come to understand it as an
unfolding process.

While the Bible and other religious literature
is very vague, there is the declaration that nothing
but "chaos" with darkness filled the void before the
beginning. It resembled a new blackboard with nothing on it. It was chaotic. If I make a mark, it is a
beginning of something. By making that mark into a
half-circle with a base, you can see the universe as
it was perceived then: "And God made the firmament,
and divided waters under the firmament from the
waters which were above the firmament" (Gen.1:7).

The word "firmament" meant just that--a divider
which was solid enough to keep the waters above the
earth from the waters which were below the earth.
This firmament explained to the ancients where "heaven" was in which God and His angels could live.

Heaven was full of light. The sun was a moving
window of heaven which ran its course during the day
and then went underground at night to race back into
the east every morning and rise again. The moon was
simply the lesser light doing the same thing. Stars
were windows of heaven; they twinkled because angels
momentarily put their heads at the windows to see if
things were going well down on earth.

Because of that cosmology, there are references
to God coming down, of temples built on hill tops to
44

be closer to heaven and of lifting up our eyes unto the hills where God might reside. We read, "I will lift up mine eyes unto the hills from whence cometh my help," (Psalms 121:1).

The story of the flood easily fits into such a cosmology. They thought of the earth as a spreading valley surrounded by the "pillars of heaven."

Since there was a universe full of water above the earth, around the earth and below the earth, the problem of having the firmament opening and water to flood down, and waters under the earth to rise up in a flood to cover the whole universe did not exist.

It was easy to accept Noah's ark and its voyage on the waters. There was no problem thinking Noah's ark came to rest upon Mt. Ararat.

Jacob's ladder reenters our thought. With that definite location for heaven above the firmament, it would be conceivable for heavenly beings to own long ladder so they could ascend and descend.

This cosmological picture fits the event of the birth of Jesus being announced by heavenly angels as they sang "from on high." It explains the heavenly dove "coming down" at His baptism; His "ascending on high" when he returned to heaven and why the disciples were "gazing up into heaven" to see Him return.

Our world-view has changed. Does this disturb our understanding of the Bible? Again, it is "yes" and "no." Changes are almost always disturbing. It does stimulate us to modernize some of our religious beliefs, but it does not destroy them. We shouldn't compel ourselves to be locked into the understanding and limited knowledge of the universe our ancestors had. They expressed their experiences with God. We should be free to express our experiences with God.

The Babylonians, Egyptians and Chinese seem to have had an understandings of the universe that was not yet known by people in the western world. However, for the purpose of this discussion, we should confine our discussions to western culture.

We discussed that until Columbus this world was still considered to be flat. The Hebrews' Babylonian captivity, commerce with Egypt, Greek philosophies, governmental power of Rome, and travels from other Mediterranean areas had enlarged the knowledge of that flatness, but it remained flat! The solid firm-

ament was still up there. A new definition was that
the ocean was not only flat, it had edges from which
a sailor could fall to his death.

The invention of the telescope and Newton's law
of gravity brought different understandings. These
brought on great conflicts, even fears, for religion
because the "firmament" was lifted from earth. This
world was no longer a cozy little land, only a mound
of dust in a huge universe. But, with the sun, moon
and stars orbiting earth, earth became thought of as
the center of the universe.

The sun was next thought to be the center. The
Earth orbited the sun. The moon circled earth; the
stars had different circuits around the sun.

Today, no one even thinks about a center of the
universe. Everything is expanding, but what it can
expand into is the next dilemma. Movements of galac-
tic systems may be specks within spiral nebulae, but
it is no longer conceivable that there is a "center"
to the universe, especially with the discovery of
those extremely distant walls of stars which had to
exist before the Big Bang's theoretical birth date.

You see, the solution to the beginning can not
be simple. What we can have, if we choose to accept
it, is a faith that no matter what or when the universe started, "In the beginning, God..."

Think about it as Gayle suggested: God is eternal. Eternity has no relationship to the passage of
time. Eternity is just the same tomorrow as it was
yesterday, or as it is today. God has an over-view
of forever, just as a satellite has an over-view of
earth which is impossible for people on the ground.

Where is God? God exists where you are, and is
where every person is. God is always everywhere.
God is also more than that: He is where every star
is; He is in the spaces between the stars; He lives
in intergalactic spaces between star systems. God is
everywhere.

Have you ever heard this expression: "The eyes
of Texas are upon you."? That has been looked at in
two ways: first, if you are a fugitive, you fear the
eyes of Texas will find you. Second, because you are
a law-abiding Texan, you feel safe and sustained by
the knowledge that you are never alone.

That is how you should feel about God.

"WHERE DOES GOD LIVE?"

"Behold, the heaven is My throne,
and the earth is My footstool."

Isaiah 66:1 and Acts 7:49

You will almost have to ignore our last discussion in order to lay a foundation for this one. You said you are constantly having someone tell you that God was "up there," or on a distant star. You have pondered the idea that God lives in individuals, not in some distant place. You have mentioned the "I AM" movement which teaches that each person is God, and that individual "gods" unite in spirit and form into a universal oneness.

Laura: "How about Colossians 1:26 and 27 which states that the mystery of the ages has been revealed unto the saints which is 'Christ in you, the hope of glory.' Isn't that like the 'I Am' teachings?"

Almost, but its meaning must be considered. If we were to read that passage with thinking that God resides only in human bodies, we would miss the importance of what Paul is saying. The "Living Bible" puts it like this: "This is the secret, that Christ in your hearts is your only hope of glory."

Paul is constantly urging people to believe in the Lord Jesus Christ to be saved. Believing in and accepting Jesus Christ is often referred to as having Christ come into your heart. He doesn't say our heart is the only dwelling place for Christ; he says that by accepting Christ salvation comes into you.

David: "That is also different from pagan idols and artifacts. As I read about pagan worship, I was made aware that they believed the gods lived within the idols and shrines. That made many millions of places where their gods lived."

Yes, we tend to localize God and the angels of heaven. One of the deep discussions throughout the middle-ages asked: "How many angels can sit upon the point of a needle?" That discussion continued going for hundreds of year. Can you answer it?

Jennifer: "You would first have to tell how big an angel is. It would be interesting to know about how big the point of a needle was then, not as sharp as today's needles, I imagine."

"Why did they not ask if God could sit on that point of a needle?" Gayle asked jokingly. "I can't believe that priests who discuss the vital religious questions, could have wasted their time that way."

"That was not a very scientific question, even with Gayle's humor." David contended. "You have two different concepts: angels are infinite; a point of a needle is definite. Infinitely small angels could make an infinitely large number--billions after billions. A point of a needle would be limited, maybe a single thousandth of an inch. Couldn't they figure that out and stop all the arguments?"

Actually, I believe they were looking for something to occupy their thinking. Religious thinkers are philosophers. The role of the philosopher is to discuss unproven theories, things of mystery. Since Religion is the greatest mystery of all, it has many philosophical theologians who really are interested in philosophizing, not with concrete facts, nor with the termination of their discussions.

Our discussion tonight is kind of philosophizing. We are considering where God might live. We see in Isaiah how God finished His comment about heaven being His throne by asking: "Where is the house you build for Me? And where is the place of My rest?"

Pagans build idols so their gods may have homes in which to live.

Animism is the belief that spirits (gods) live in water, rocks, brooks, birds, animals and in all natural things.

"When the Russian astronauts circled the earth they declared that there was no God because they had looked everywhere but did not discover 'heaven.' If they believed as they were taught, why did they even bother to look?" Jesse asked.

Just because Russia proclaimed there was no God did not stop the people of Russia from continuing to believe that there was a God.

Carl Jung, the psychology student under Freud, wrote that there is a universal urge toward perfection surging through our unconsciousness. He did not give a name to his "cosmic urge," probably because a conditioning of rigid Freudian atheism--total rejection that there might be a God--made him fearful of revealing his true thoughts. Freud liked to say, "I am the master of my own fate." People who declare themselves to be the masters of their lives, often become aggressively defensive. This can happen within religion, and with persons having no religion.

Because you'll be bombarded with many different ideas about where God might be, it seems appropriate to take time to discuss some of them to see how they stand up to the criteria of God being a spirit, and the discussion we just had about where God is.

"I don't understand the problem," Laura protested. "Everybody knows that God lives in heaven."

That is just the point, Laura. There isn't any agreement on what heaven means. But we will be discussing what heaven is in another discussion.

For tonight, let us look at our charts. Where do they say God lives?

Jesse: "You must be referring to the space just above the firmament. We know there isn't any such a place, just as we pointed out about the Russian cosmonauts looking all around the earth to find it. I have come to understand that God sometimes speaks in figurative terms, not in strict scientific language. Jesus spoke to people using parables, similes, with illustrations or stories. Shouldn't we accept that where God lives can only be given allegorically?"

"Maybe that's something of what Paul meant when he wrote in First Corinthians, 11:13, 'When I was a child, I spake as a child, but when I became a man I put away childish things,'" Jennifer offered.

Good, we do change our thinking as we grow into adult life. Wouldn't this be a boring life if facts without changes were all we ever knew? Where would be the excitement of discovering new truths?

You all helped reassemble the jumble of letters I wrote on the board, **"GODISNOWHERE."** Think about a deduction we should have made at that time: when we stated that God is no "where," we also said He can't need a "place" to stay. It is easy to let our minds vacillate between physical and spiritual concepts of God. Swinging between opposing ideas usually causes a great amount of confusion and fear.

    One of the techniques of debaters is to confuse
a speaker by asking questions with dual or ambiguous
meanings. Take this ancient story told about a fool
who cupped a little bird in his hands and brought it
before a wise man. The fool asked: "Is this little
bird alive or dead?" The fool believed that he had
given the wise man an impossible question. When the
wise man would answer that the bird was alive, the
fool could merely tighten his grip to kill the bird;
but if the wise man replied that the bird was dead,
the fool would open his hands and let the bird fly
free. After a moment the wise man answered: "It is
as you wish it to be."

    Religious controversies often resemble the tale
of the little bird. Attempting to handle dilemmas,
we create confusion or become lost in uncertainties.

    Skeptics love to question Christians to confuse
them with things which have no definite answers, and
with questions which are known to be contentions.

    An old saying declares that any fool may ask a
question which even the wisest sage can not answer.
Accept the bait and you will be ridiculed since the
questioner knows both sides of the dilemma and will
proclaim your ignorance. The skeptic will have won
the victory.

    The book of Proverbs advises us: "Answer not a
fool according to his folly, lest thou also be like
unto him" (Prov. 26:4). The next verse is similar:
"Answer a fool according to his folly, lest he be
wise in his own conceit" (Prov. 26:5). In the first
verse is the warning that to mingle with unbelievers
will cause you to become an unbeliever. Another old
saying puts it this way: a barrel of apples becomes
spoiled with the presence of a single rotten one.

    The second verse says that if you argue with a
fool all you will accomplish is helping the fool to
think himself to be wiser than you are. You can not
convince a fool that he is wrong. If you attempt to
argue religion with a fool who thinks himself to be
wise, you will only convince him of his own wisdom.

    We need to have answers for our faith, but when
we believe that God is everywhere, there is no sense
in arguing about where He lives. Getting tangled in
unexplainable dogmas, we could find ourselves ridiculed; we also begin to doubt our own faith.
50

Jesus did not demand college educations to follow Him. He did not require a university degree to go out and tell others about His salvation and love. All He requested was that disciples speak out and to witness to what they had experienced.

I will never forget the experience I had being in a group of scoffers in Central Park, Los Angeles. The park afforded an opportunity for all beliefs to be espoused. Attempting to witness about Jesus was sure to get an argument. I was challenged by a loud voice saying: "If you are so smart, answer me this: when a wave breaks upon a shore, does the water move or is there something else causing the wave action?" I did not know the answer; he used this technique so often that he knew he had the upper hand. He yelled at me until I felt like a dog which had been beaten and had run away with its tail between its legs.

It is not necessary to know everything, but it is necessary that you have a communicative knowledge of your belief. We Christians should not expect to be in agreement upon all things, there are too many thoughts about God. Because I believe that God is a spirit and is "omnipresent," I can be comfortable in believing that God does not need a home--His home is everywhere.

One more thought: our concept of "heaven" is of a place of eternal glory, isn't it? We also have a belief that the eternal God is glorious. What could be more logical than to say that to be in "glory" is to be in the presence of God? This reasons out that heaven is where God is--and God is everywhere!

Jesus said that the Kingdom of Heaven is now at hand (Matt. 34:17). Since the Kingdom of Heaven is where God is, then Jesus must have been saying that God is where you are, and where every person is. No space divides God from us.

King David, the Psalmist, pondered the awesomeness of God and wrote: "Whither shall I go from Thy spirit? Or whither shall I flee from Thy presence?

"If I ascend into heaven, Thou art there: if I make my bed in hell, behold, Thou art there.

"If I take the wings of the morning, and dwell in the uttermost parts of the sea, Thou art there."

Psalms 139: 7-10 continues, "Even there shall Thy hand lead me, and Thy right hand shall hold me."

"I need to change my thinking," Laura said. "I have not thought of God as being far from us, but it is hard to visualize God as being everywhere."

It took me a long time to accept this concept. Actually, I guess I will always be adventuring into the mysteries of God.

"But can't we ever reach a place where we don't have to struggle anymore?" Laura responded.

I hope not. Struggles give us challenges.It is possible that it isn't the struggle you are protesting, but the lack of directions to help you in your struggle. You did your home-work in school in order to get good grades; you rejoiced as you received the grades you wanted. Teachers could not take your test for you, but they could give you guidance and help.

School is an experience of constantly unfolding of new vistas, rejecting the challenge could result in becoming a drop-out. You struggled then just to be alive. Ceasing to struggle is death.

Knowledge provides you with tools to help make the struggle easier. Knowledge of God can make your journey of life more meaningful and fulfilling. You can be a religious dropout and never attain strength from the abundant power of God. As a dropout, you can never know the magnitude of your own potentials.

The struggle for self-actualization never ends because you have no help stronger than yourself.

That is where your relationship with God comes in, and why it is important for you to accept God.

You have heard me say this before: "don't have too small a God." If your God is too limited, your expanse of life will be just that restricted. Your success with life will be just that tiny since your happiness will have nothing to sustain it.

Here is another thought from a church bulletin:
**"Happiness is not getting what you want,
But wanting what you have."**

Selfish people are always wanting more and more from life. They can never be filled. They are like a desert which never has enough water. The desert's happiness is in knowing the value of itself, not in yearning to be a tropical garden which it cannot be.

The presence of God in your life enables you to recognize your own values and rejoice that you are such an esteemed child of God.

52

WHAT DOES GOD LOOK LIKE?

"No man hath seen God at any time."

1 John 4:12

Jennifer: "I asked the question because my Sunday School teacher used to tell us that God looked like Santa Claus, only not so fat or rosy. She also said that if I could find an old man with gray hair and a long beard I would be seeing someone who resembled God."

"Not only that," Jesse continued, "I've read a lot about man-made images which are given the titles of being gods. Idols are called gods; some of these look like birds, or animals, or half human and half-animal. The emperor of Japan was considered to be a god. The Tibetan Dalai Lama is considered to be the personification or reincarnation of God. Is he what God looks like?"

You have left out many other people who worship the sun, the moon, the planets and other stars. As we discussed in our first session, people have worshipped almost everything in nature including trees, weather, pretty stones, rivers, lakes, mountain formations and hills. We said that we would be using a small "g" in reference to man-created gods, but God does not look like these "gods."

Jennifer: "There are many people who think that God has a human form. In fact, the Bible reveals He does human things such as walking with Adam and Eve in the Garden of Eden, talking to Moses out from the burning bush, making prophets cover their eyes so as not to be blinded if they looked upon His glory, and appearing as a dove at Jesus' baptism. He sits upon His throne in heaven. Some Scripture passages indicate that God is a human form--didn't He create Adam to have His own likeness?

I have to confess that when I was in my 'teens I was taught that God looked like a man--or that the physical form of man was the likeness of God. When I

was in Sunday School I worked hard to merit those
extra stars which were to be placed on my crown in
heaven. The number of stars would indicate the position that I would be given.

Of course, I wanted to be as near to that glorious golden throne of God as possible. I wanted a
mansion prepared for me in heaven so I'd be on the
golden street, just across from God's temple. A harp
of gold would enable me to play music for the angels
of heaven. I wanted everything!

As I look back, it seems to me that I was being
taught a very selfish religion.

Remember, we have proposed to avoid human doctrines about religion, so what I just said shouldn't
be taken as a denial of the rights of people to form
their own concepts about God.

We have discussed that people can only begin to
journey toward God from whatever belief they now are
holding God. Variations exist. It is important that
we allow others to have the freedom of belief which
we desire for ourselves.

The human eye is incapable of seeing God. However, because of our inquisitive minds, we would go
mad if we were denied the right to formulate neither
a positive nor a negative concept about God.

We create images of things which we haven't yet
seen. Think of all the artists of the world who try
to paint Jesus. Jesus has been depicted as Oriental
or occidental. He has been painted as Roman, Anglo-
Saxon, African, Eskimo, Mexican, Indian, Russian or
Italian--and even Jewish, His own family heritage.

He has been pictured as a joyful person, a man
of sorrows, one who knew grief and pain. He is pictured as being tall, short, fat, slender, strong or
weak. You have never seen Jesus, but don't you have
in your mind some type of visual image of Him? The
more I read the Bible and tried to match its imagery
to its definitions the more confused I became.

I would read some verse--then I would ask:
"God is love." What does love look like?
"God is a spirit." What does a spirit look
like?
"God is eternal." How old would He appear?
"God is everywhere." What kind of shape would
God have in order to be everywhere? How can He
54

see this side of the earth and the other side
all at the same time? Will I be everywhere when
I arrive into heaven? I didn't even understand
what I was asking.

Paul's letter to the Galatians says that there
are no racial differences in heaven: there's neither
Jew nor Greek; there are no power classes nor caste
systems; there is neither slave nor free; and there
are no gender differences--there are no male nor female persons (Gal. 3:28).

What would God look like with no racial charac-
teristic? What kind of leadership would God have if
there are no political organizations? How could you
distinguish God from anyone else if everyone getting
into heaven looks exactly like Him?

That was a joke. Why are you not laughing? Was
it serious?

If Paul was correct when he wrote there is neither
male nor female, and we will grant that he was, then
God must be neither male nor female! What would God
look like without being male or female? Diving gear
and other clothing can make us seem to be without a
gender, but that doesn't answer our question.

"You're confusing us." Laura protested. "I am
sure there is a God, but what you are implying seems
to be that there is no God, or that 'God' is but an
idea."

Thanks, Laura. I am not trying to confuse you,
only to get you to be thinking out some of the logic
of the Bible. As I've said before, I see the Bible
as being logical. I believe God is always practical
as well as incomprehensibly mystical. He displayed
His practicality when He led the Israelites out from
Egypt and into the desert. God understood that they
would be hungry and thirsty, so He sent them bread.
He knew they would be thirsty: He made water to gush
from a rock.

When they made complaints about the bland diet,
He gave them meat. It is astounding how many refer-
ences to His humanness there are in the Bible. And
He is always that great Incomprehensible Mystery.

The book of Psalms shows David recognizing the
mystical presence of God. The book of Job portrays
that mystical power. Jesus was the personification
of the mysterious God. Paul's vision on the road to

Damascus was a mystical experience, as was the roof-
top experience Peter had when a sheet with all kinds
of meats was let down from heaven before him and he
was told to eat of even the unclean meat. He understood the message to be that the gospel of Christ be
given even to the gentiles.

When you read your Bible, leave your mind open
to recognize how the mystical God moves in this very
practical world. My only warning would be not to be
so heavenly oriented that you are no earthly good.

One of the ways God speaks to Man is in dreams.
The dream may have mystical communication, or it may
be interpreted in many other ways without religious
meanings. God speaks, and is heard the same as any
other voice is heard. He makes Himself known through
"feelings." He can be seen as He displays His power
by manipulating the forces of nature such as He did
when Jesus stilled the raging storm. We pray for a
better life and He changes things. But, He does not
show His face!

David: "Is that why so many scientists declare
there is no proof of God? Don't some psychologists
use the same arguments you have just stated to prove
that all of our thoughts about God are psychological
phenomenon? Why doesn't God just make Himself seen
and end all this bickering?"

He appeared in Jesus. Did the life of Jesus remove doubts about the reality of God? Almost immediately after Jesus went into heaven, intellectuals,
Gnostics and humanists were declaring the Disciples
merely gathered together some valuable sociological
truths from other religions and put them together
into what they called "Christianity." In fact, the
Gospel of John, the last one written, is thought by
some theologians to have been written by some mystic
to counteract those attempts to depersonalize Jesus.

The Gospel of John is the most mystical writing
in the whole Bible about the amazing love of God.

God's love is vastly different from human love.

When people looked at Jesus, did they see God?
That's a catch question.

"Aren't there many historical documentations of
people who have seen images of Jesus, or some other
religious figure?" responded Gayle. "I have read of
such experiences."

There have been many such incidences, but there
have always been scoffers rejecting such experiences
as mental delusions or strange shadows which play on
the imagination. God can not be a proven to be a
"scientific" fact, so it is easy for scoffers to say
there is nothing real in a mystical experience.

Your own experience, Gayle, is a lesson in how
others will deny you ever had such an experience, it
was real to you, however.

Jesus discussed the nature of God with a group
of Rabbis who had questioned Him. With an exchange
of ideas, Jesus replies: "Not that any man hath seen
the Father, save he which is of God, he hath seen
the Father" (John 4:46). Do you suppose they understood Him? They surely did not openly accept Him.

Jesus said that no ordinary man could see God,
but that He had seen the Father because He was from
God. You have to understand that "Jehovah," "God,"
and "Lord" are used interchangeably in the Bible.

We will discuss the various names of God later.

Jesus had a discussion with Philip in which He
discussed that whosoever has seen Him has also seen
the Father (John 14:1-9). However, Philip will not
be satisfied with psychological or mystical answers
which may be just talk; he wants physical manifestations. Read Jesus' answer: "Have I been so longtime
with you, and hast thou not known me, Philip? He
that has seen Me has seen the Father, henceforth ye
know Him, and have seen Him."

Do you think that when you arrive in heaven you
will see God in the physical form of Jesus? Nations
into which Christianity has entered pictures Him in
their ethnic image.

We have read Paul's statement stating neither
Jew nor Greek, male nor female will be identified as
such in heaven. It may be there is something Jesus
and Paul were saying about what heaven is like which
is difficult to comprehend with our physical minds.

When we use the phrase "I see," we are stating
that we understand; we are not referring to the activity of the eyes. We also say "I hear you," and we
are referring to comprehending what you said, not to
hearing with our ears. The mind acts in ways which
may not involve physical actions. Such actions of
the mind can not measured by science.

Because psychiatrists haven't another terminology for unusual occurrences, they refer to receiving thoughts as ESP (Extra-Sensory Perception). It also is called a "sixth sense." People with ESP or the "sixth sense" are called "psychic"; they can receive other people's thoughts, and sometimes become aware of distant events.

Could it be that "psychic" receptions are really communications leaking out from the ever-present and universal spirit of God?

If an ignorant aborigine of Australia or Africa had a radio, but had no knowledge how it functioned, and knew nothing of the radio station which sent out signals for that radio, the aborigine might think of the radio as something magic. Maybe the radio would be thought to have ESP! It might even be worshipped as if it were some religious manifestation.

The world is full of soothsayers, mind-readers, fortune tellers, prognosticators and fore-tellers of the future. Some claim to have power in themselves; others claim have communications coming from astral beings; some claim to receive communications from a dead spirit. Many famous people have had a private astrologist or psychic advisor.

Why should we refuse to believe God's spiritual communications? We are blinded by charlatans, con-artists and other exploiters. Some even declare they have religious powers.

It is almost impossible to find the truth amid the noise and confusions of commercial programs and denominational differences. It is difficult to find a consistent basis for our faith. How desperate we become to find the truth which will set us free such as Jesus talked about (John 8:32).

Now, you tell me what God looks like.

Laura, " From what you have been saying, it may be that the question of what God looks like could be the wrong question. Not 'wrong' because we are forbidden to ask it, but wrong from the perspective of human experiences."

"I don't know," Gayle continued. "Our concept of what we will be when we get to heaven seems pertinent to how we expect to see God. If I am expecting some human shape, be able to shake your hand, eat a bowl of soup with you and climb the highest

mountain with you, wear dresses, get my hair fixed
in some beauty salon or do other physical activities
or have close relationships with you in heaven, I'll
be expecting God to be like that.

"That's what the American Indians expected when
they died and went to their 'Happy Hunting Ground,'
especially if they died as a great warrior," David
added.

Laura again: "Is that not similar to the concept of heaven that the ancient Hebrews had when the
Old Testament was being written? Isn't the portrayal
of Jacob's ladder related to a physical heaven which
is just a little way above the earth? The expression
that God looked down from heaven also expresses that
physical heaven."

Your observation, Laura, is correct. However,
let us hold our discussion about heaven until later.

Jennifer, you thought you had asked a question
which could be answered easily. Look where we have
gone! There isn't any simple answer because of the
complexities of Man's meager understand of the realm
of the spirit. Paul said that we look at the kingdom
of God as through a glass which is clouded.

Let me share with you my own conclusions. God
is a spirit. Spirit is a term like atmosphere. You
do not see the air, but you know it is here--and it
is there. You can grasp the idea of air encircling
the earth. Extensive as it is, it is essential for
it to be where you are and abundantly available with
you at all times.

That is somewhat the way I envision God. It is
not that I can "see" Him with my physical eyes, but
He infuses my spirit and "I see" that He is with me.
Just as the air has the faculty of being in me without lessening its ability to be with every other individual, so I believe that the universality of God
and the eternality of His existence puts Him both in
our physical universe and the transcendental, everlasting realm of "heaven."

Consider the idea of meeting with your beloveds
when your earthly life is transformed into heavenly
life. What will those who entered heaven before you
look like? Will they have grown older? Will children
have grown into adults? Will disabled or aged people
be restored to their health and youthful conditions?

Mothers may want to hold their baby, but the babies
may have grown to become mothers who want their own
babies to hold. I am not trying to be funny. I just
wanted to point out how impossible it is to make a
dogmatic determination about life beyond the grave.
All we can be sure of is that it will be far more
glorious than we can picture in earthly terms.

The Bible talks about knowing our loved ones by
their spirit--by their love. There won't be any more
sickness, no more poverty, no more wars, no domestic
conflicts, no smog, earthquakes, fires or floods, no
jealousies or hatreds. All things will be different
when we inherit the perfect love of God.

Love has no shape or limitation. God is without
shape or limitation. God is love.

Throughout Man's history God has been revealing
Himself as much as Man was able to comprehend. Isn't
it obvious that our ideas about heaven are pictured
in terminologies of our physical understandings?

Defining God seals Him within that description.
There is no shame in imagining God to be so glorious
that human words cannot define Him.

I challenge you: think about the abundant love
you will experience when you meet God face-to-face.
You don't need a definition. All you need is great
expectations of an existence far beyond our ability
to imagine.

When you come to the presence of Perfect Love,
you will see God.

Live today with such a spiritual openness that
the perfect love of God can be in you. "The Kingdom
of Heaven is at hand," Jesus told the disciples. He
continued by saying that the Kingdom of Heaven is
within you; that you participate in Eternal Life the
moment you commit your life to the salvation He came
to provide.

Gayle added: "I understand that. When I had my
experience of closeness to God, I experienced Him in
my spirit. He didn't have any shape, but I saw His
presence. I knew I was enfolded in His everlasting
arms."

And, feeling enfolded in the loving arms of God
is a good place to close this session.

WHO IS GOD?

"I am that I am!"
Exodus 3:14

Gayle: "Just after our discussion I found this copy of the December, 1990, issue of LIFE. Look at the cover. It is blank except for the question: 'WHO IS GOD?' Can we discuss what LIFE had to say about God?"

It makes us depart a bit from our goal of looking at God from an uncluttered view-point, but maybe it will tell us something about God. Have the rest of you read it? Let's divide it and take some time so all of us can read it.

Ready? Then, Gayle, why don't you start us off with your feelings about the entire article?

"Mostly, I thought it was overly displayed with a cover like that. There was no cohesiveness and no conclusion. It was a collection of the opinions of many individuals thinking about God. I have found a few intriguing points, however, which I hope we will be able to discuss."

Jesse: "While disappointed with the article for lacking any certainties, I guess it illustrates that God can not be defined by LIFE, nor by any persons or groups of persons."

That's a logical observation. Let's go on with the individuals' thoughts and see if they contribute meanings to our discussion.

"To start with, the prelude states: 'Witnesses come from divergent traditions; the God they worship goes by many names. Yet He is always looking upon His creatures with a steady compassion, a God who has no trouble contemplating the face of us.' That's most impressive, but it does not seem like very good grammar at the end," was Gayle's remark.

"The first person, a lady who is dying when she is 67, thinks about death and God. She says: 'What if there really is a God?' Then she says 'I am almost sure He is there.' She feels His presence, is cocooned in His love, yet she can't come out with a

positive confidence in God. I sure wish she could
have had more of an assurance about her relationship to God," Laura observed. "I hope that when I
get older I will have a more positive feeling about
dying. Will there come a time when people will know
they should experience God without fear?"

Jesse: "I thought the African Archbishop's idea
about God being always present with us was good, but
when he expressed his concerns about God letting the
Jews in Germany be tortured, I wanted him to present
a some kind of an explanation. It seemed that there
was still a lot of anger inside of him about why God
does not just wiped way inhuman conduct. Will we be
talking about that sometime?"

Yes, Jesse, that subject is scheduled for about
a month from now. You can prepare by thinking about
God creating us in His likeness, with the freedom to
love Him. This also gives us the freedom not to love
Him. We will discuss the origin of evil in a couple
of weeks.

Laura, you are almost the same age as the next
witness. What did you think of her?

"Her's is a lovely story. I do not understand
her logic, however. She ends by stating that up in
heaven everyone will be the same color, black. However. in the beginning she seems to be rejecting the
fact that she is black. If heaven changes everyone
into black people, the best color on earth should be
black. It was interesting to see how humanistic she
made God, and how earthly she thought heaven to be."

The next one carries your name, David. What do
you think about a murderer becoming a Christian?

"He expressed an intellectual belief, but I can
not see that he had any experience with God," David
responds. "He still feels guilty, but not forgiven.
His prayer shows that he is still wanting to justify
himself. I can relate to that. I am full of my own
ambitions, but I am hoping that I can be willing to
accept God's directions for my life."

Jennifer: "The little child is next. She says
what many people expect of God. I know persons who
expect God to manipulate their slot-machines of life
just so they could always win. They get angry with
God when He does not control all the machines for
them.

62

"I suppose the author was intending to show us a very childish opinion of God."

Did the next one say anything to you, Jennifer?

"It reminded me of my own life. I have always been certain that I was in love whenever I got a new boy-friend, but now that I have dropped those boys I have a difficult time recalling the ecstacy I had at that time. I do not have that feeling about Jesse, and he recognizes it, but we do have a close friendship.

"Maybe I'm like that journalist who doesn't go to church because he can't recover the intimate and pleasing feeling about God he experienced while facing death at the hands of Muslim terrorists. Is it true that we can't force God into intimacy with us?"

We cannot force God, but we can open our hearts to Him. It is something like a hypnotist attempting to put to sleep a very resistant person. The hypnotist cannot get through a shut mind. The concept of free-will says that God does not force Himself upon us if we close our hearts against Him.

The article about the Arab terrorist amazed me. He was so frank in expressing his Moslem faith. The pleadings of the World Council of Churches that non-Arabs accept the Islamic religion as a peace-seeking religion equal to Christianity bothers me. It stated that all religions had peaceful and loving Gods, but this Arab would deny peace to those outside of his own faith. You recall that Khomeini took over Iran and slaughtered those who opposed him.

Mohammed Ali, the boxer, changed to Mohammedism because he considered it more humane and loving than Christianity!

LIFE printed the terrorist's declaration about there being a 'Holy War' to please Allah by killing off those who are not Mohammedans. LIFE'S terrorist sees a vengeful God being in a war between Right and Wrong, Justice and Injustice. To him, non-believers are evil: they must be killed to the glory of Allah, and that he, as a good Mohammedan agent of Allah, is commissioned to kill infidel non-believers.

The terrorist declares the universe to have but one Master, and that all humans are His slaves. The same picture of God is present in most of the Near-East.

Much of Africa is accepting Mohammedism. Is it because it offers a religious reason for killing off their enemies?

Your belief about God, you see, greatly decides your relationships to your fellow-man.

"How about the gay minister who has AIDS?" asks Laura. "It seems to me that he is defending his way of life as he condemns Anita Bryant when she said on Phil Donahue's show that gays needed conversion into the love of God.

"However, he is not so sure of himself with his closing remarks where he shows a self-rejection. He bemoans his fate with: 'God, I have been a good and faithful servant to you, why did you do this to me? But I realized that God understood what I was feeling. God did not give this to me. God was crying and was right beside me. God was greater than AIDS. God heals.' I can't help wondering if he was crying out because he was gay, or was he lashing out because he considered himself to have been a good and faithful minister who deserved protection and should not have contracted AIDS?"

What was the minister's picture of God? Can we see the face of God through this man? You'll profit by on one thing the minister said: "God was crying." Laura also told us of God's tears a while back.

There is the beggar of India who declared that he has never sinned, but that he must have sinned in a previous life and is now fated to pay the penalty for that sin. He sees God, Brahma, as having judged his fate. He cries out, "God is vengeful. He really punishes. There is no escape from the consequences of sin. I pray that heaven is better than this." He does not see God as being very loving.

This is this religion which Hinduism is aggressively introducing into America and Europe.

I repeat, how God appears to you determines how you will live your own life as well as how you will live in relationship to other people. That is why we are taking two sessions to discuss who God is, along with what He looks like.

I would like to terminate this discussion about LIFE's article by observing that the author does not consolidate the witnesses to make some kind of logic to the article. Rather, he ignores the witnesses to give his own observation about God as being allusive and elusive.

Did any of you understand what he meant? Will you help us, Gayle? We need you to help by defining those words.

"I can't put words into the author's mouth, but allusive means something which is casual or indirect and ethereal. It has the sense of being desirable, but untouchable. Allusive as he used it, can relate to allure and allude. Elusive is that which is baffling or improbable, difficult to grasp; it is like a face behind a thick veil," Gayle responded.

As the "Supreme Allusive-Elusive," God would be a great quandary. The author goes on to write that God alone knows what He is doing. "All we can do," he says, "is to let God do His thing."

"I must keep my mouth shut and accept what God does without attempting to understand," he wrote.

Let me leave LIFE's article and tell an ancient story from India. You may have heard this story as if it were a recent invention, but it was written in the Vedas of pre-Buddha India.

The story tells of six blind men who come to a very wise guru and ask what an elephant looked like. The wise man knew if he described the elephant as he saw it, the blind men would have no comprehension of the animal. Therefore, he told the men to touch the elephant.

The first man touched the tail, then exclaimed: "Aha, now I know, the elephant looks like a rope."

The second man felt the elephant's side and responded: "Aha, now I know! The elephant is not like a rope, but like a great wall."

The third blind man put his arms around a leg. He exclaimed: "Aha! Now I know. It is not a rope or a wall, but it is like a great tree."

The fourth man explored an ear. "Aha," he cried out. "Now I know! The elephant does not resemble a rope, a wall or a tree. It is a huge lotus leaf."

The fifth blind man was helped to feel the elephant's trunk. He felt all the way to the end just as the elephant shot water out. "Aha, now I have an understanding of the elephant. It isn't like a rope, a wall, a tree or a lotus leaf, but it is like a big pipe with water running out. I am sure because I ex-

perienced the flow of water. You should all know as
I do that this is what an elephant is," he exulted.

Lastly, the sixth man touched the tusk. "Now I
know! The elephant is not a rope, nor a wall, nor a
tree, nor a lotus leaf and not a pipe, but is a pole
of hard stone pointed at the end," he announced.

Which of the blind men knew the truth? Each of
them knew the truth as they had experienced it. The
problem was that they had no way of sharing with the
others, so they were limited to know only that part
they had individually touched. Even had they shared
what they had experienced, they would have had only
a partial understanding of the entire elephant.

Which of the numerous different religions tell
what God looks like? Each of them, in part.

God shows Himself, but can only be experienced
through the limitations of an individual person, or
a group of persons or a society.

God always rejects evil, so He would be seen by
evil persons as stern and unrelenting. On the other
hand, persons who accepts God's love and forgiveness
would see Him reaching out with His love to seek and
to save those who are lost.

It is not that religions and beliefs about God
are wrong, but that Man has such a limited ability
to understand spiritual things it has been next to
impossible to consolidate the differing revelations
of God into a composite, unified whole.

My ego wants my concept of God to be His actual
reality and truth. Your ego wants your knowledge of
God be the only true and complete revelation. Most
of you have experienced God; you know that what you
believe is true. When the apostle Paul experienced
God he allowed the insights and revelations to expand his life so he would better understand God and
be prepared to relate to people.

Let us read First Corinthians, 11:13. "When I
was a child, I spake as a child; but when I became a
man I put away childish things."

To you, God looks like what you imagine Him to
look like. Beware that you do not make your God too
small.

God's definition of Himself states: "I am that
'I am'!" There are at least 600 times in the Bible
where God refers to Himself as: "I am the Lord."

There is no arrogance or bragging with God. He simply states what He is. But, the totality of what He is is beyond our greatest imaginations.

God's statement was in response to people chasing after rumors and making claims about who God is. They made idols, and images and worshipped all sorts of animal and humanistic shapes. Idols are endowed by their worshippers with thoughts and utterances so the idol seems to claim: "I am god."

God answers those boasts decisively as He declares that He is the only one who is eligible to announce: "I am that which all others claim they are." (That is my paraphrasing of "I am that I am.")

Gayle: "I get excited when I think of God being over the entire universe. The problem I had when I was a youth was wanting a God here on earth, not out in the immensity of space. I was hesitant of saying anything to friends who had studied the stars or had seen microscopic life as they studied biology, genetics, geology and other sciences. With an expanding vision of God, these little discoveries into the how and wherefor of creation no longer bother me. I can even envision God as being pleased with those urges to delve into the mysteries of creation. After all, God does not need to keep secrets. He certainly did not create a brain within us just to have us be like stupid clay dolls."

My facetiousness comes in here, Gayle. Pardon the levity, but recalling your spiritual growth made me think of TV's ad: "You've come a long way, baby."

Who is God? When I read the Bible I often see apparent humor in the way God reveals Himself.

David was but an ignorant shepherd boy when God called him out to fight against the foe who had sent torrents of fear running through the Israelites. No Israelite soldier could challenge the giant Goliath. I can almost hear David protesting: "Who? Me! You've got to be joking!" I can imagine the soldiers being amazed at the apparent bragging of this boy offering to fight the giant; they probably laughted at him.

David went before the king who was in deep despair because he was faced with defeat. Can you feel a sense of comic drama as the king loaded upon that little boy all the heavy armor of a strong soldier? David had never worn anything heavier than a robe.

The armor revealed that the king did not think God could do anything without full battle gear. Just Imagine David falling to the floor with that weight.

Learn this proverb: "Man's despair is God's opportunity."

David faced the giant. Soldiers offered lances and war-clubs, but David calmly picked up a rounded stone from the creek, put it in his sling, and faced the giant. Goliath roared with laughter; jeers came from the enemy camp. Did God quietly smile as David hurled the stone and slew Goliath?

Why didn't God just go out and slay Goliath?

Who is God? He's the source of Man's strength. He gives us freedom to fight our own battles, but we can be victorious in life only when we are following what He has directed us to do.

"How about all the rich and powerful people who do not follow God?" asked David.

They are not forgotten. Jesus answered in this manner: "What shall it profit a man, if he gain the whole world, and lose his own soul?" (Mark 8:36).

There are many passage which give this thought: "Be not deceived; God is not mocked: for whatsoever a man soweth, that shall he also reap."

"For he that soweth of his flesh shall of the flesh reap corruption; but he that soweth to the Spirit shall of the Spirit reap life everlasting" (Galatians 6:7,8).

One other thought: life is a gamble, nothing is certain. Christ offers an insurance policy against losing eternity. When you take out a life-insurance policy you are betting that you could have an early death. The insurance company bets on your living to a ripe old age. The facetious and horribly possible comment says that if you have faith in God and there is a heaven to gain, you win; but if you reject God and trust in your strength, you not only lose living a meaningful and loving life and your reward will be the grave and eternal rejection from heaven.

ARE THERE DIFFERENT IDEAS ABOUT WHO GOD IS?

"Whom do men say that I the Son of Man am?"
Matthew 16:16

Would you believe that over twenty-five hundred years ago a great religious leader of India declared there must be over two million gods in India?

Every group of people throughout Man's history has developed some idea about powers beyond the life of humanity, Gods have been envisioned as horrible and destructive, as well as benevolent, caring gods. In our earlier discussion we talked about the multitude of objects, nature's forces, animals, heavenly bodies, and special persons as being gods.

Ancient Greeks thought the gods were similar to humans, but lived longer and lived beyond the world. These gods often fell in love with some beautiful or handsome person of earth, married the humans and had children who became the "heroes" of legends. These children were called "demi-gods."

Greek gods had emotions and weaknesses similar to humans. They had drunken parties, they had conflicts of roles, were jealous of other gods, fought battles with earthly animals for sport or to protect their home, Mt. Olympus. They seemed to enjoy bouts with humans, and fighting to protect humans from the mystical giants and gods who terrorized the earth.

Each god had individual powers: Neptune was god of the sea, Athena was goddess of earth, Hercules, a god of wrath, hurled thunderbolts upon erring humans on earth, Zeus was head of the gods, and was thought by some Greek theologians to have been the father of the other gods.

The Romans, also, had numerous gods, including Caesar. This caused enmity with Christians who refused to pay honor to Caesar as a god. Rome allowed the religions of conquered people to be worshipped, but they were compelled to worship Caesar first. It was allowable to worship Jesus, but the trouble was that Christians refused to give homage to Caesar.

Jehovah's Witnesses see themselves as upholding the law of not bowing before any national god, nor any emblem. They consider the flag to be an image. Saluting the flag, paying homage to a nation, giving allegiance or making any other form of commitment to a government would be in direct disobedience to the commandment of God that there shall be no other gods before Him. Witnesses are in almost every country of the world, but they see themselves belonging only to the universal Kingdom of Jehovah. They also reject Jesus on that same basis. Although they think of Him a teacher, they believe that He was just a human and must not be worshipped.

Jesse asks: "What about all the people who are afraid of God? Our discussion theme is that there is no fear in God. Psalms mentions "fear" of the Lord. 'He will bless them that fear the Lord, both small and great' (Psalms 114:13). I looked up Paul's admonition in Acts 13:26: 'Whosoever among you feareth God, to you is the word of salvation sent.' I have not looked them all up, but I understand there are many passages in both the Old and New Testaments which admonish fear of the Lord."

" And how about all the native people of primitive countries who build their whole religious practices around being afraid," David adds. "My studies of ancient religions showed them to be more involved in fearing their gods than in loving them."

Actually, we have been commenting on different things. Being afraid is a primary human emotion. We Wonder about supernatural powers and involve a basic human emotion. "Fear" is used both to express fright and reverence.

Actually, I have heard psychiatrists say it is easier to make people afraid than to bring them into a position of trust and peace. Since God is thought by many people to control the uncontrollable forces of nature, Man grows more aware of negative emotions than of positive ones.

Fear of the dark is universal. Darkness is seen as holding all the unknown factors and powers which could harm us. People without an experience of God's love and care develop a fear response to life and to the universe. Because there are many unknown things which generate fear, it was natural to have a god of

70

each fear. It never mattered that self-made gods had no power.

On the other hand, the verse which says: "Fear of the Lord is the beginning of wisdom," means to be respectful of God. References to fear in the Psalms usually refer to honoring God and being faithful to Him. We've already discussed the difference between fear as "awe,' and fear as being afraid.

Ancient Hindus with their millions of gods had a belief that there was only one Supreme Creator, or Motivator, Vishnu. While all other gods will be gone at the end of a life-cycle of a universe, Vishnu has to remain because he is the Eternally Divine Principle, the Ultimate Reality. He is not in time.

Buddhists deny the existence of Vishnu, Brahma, and any concept of a universal or eternal entity. An individual must grow into consciousness of the inner self, the inner god.

A book from The Buddhist Lodge of London, England, includes the question about whether they are atheists. The book, WHAT IS BUDDHISM?, responded to like this: "If by 'atheist' you mean one who rejects the concept of a personal God, we are." It goes on to explain: "It is just as reasonable to think of a universe regulated by a Law as it is to think of a distant Personage who is not seen; who dwells in a place nobody knows; who began a universe from nothingness; who caused an earth to be inhabited by entities which make endless strife, suffering, poverty, wars and other sorts of social injustices."

Buddhists, you see, are like other people who are compelled to deny the existence of God because they cannot deal with the question of evil. You may hear the question: "If there is a God, why did He allow evil to get started--why doesn't He do something to get rid of it?"

There are three basic sects of Buddhism which all ask: "How can I escape these rebirths back into suffering humanity?"

Buddhism's concern is how to attain nirvana, an eternal bliss of unawareness. Such a concern points to Buddha as being self-centered.

Jesus said, "Do unto others as you would that others do unto you." This is the Christian "Golden Rule." The "rule" is similar to Buddha's. Here is

71

what he admonished: "Do not do unto others what you do not want done unto yourself."

"Karma," or "fate," is the center of Buddhism: Man has no choice, but is fated to live a life pre-determined by previous existences. We see almost the same thought in Christianity's predestination which says that God created the universe, set it going by a definite pattern, then went away and rested, having no more to do it.

"Does that mean these people only believe they are praying?" asked Jesse. "It seems to me that if God decreed that I pray at such and such a time, and had already set in motion the answers to my prayers, then I am not really praying--I'm only being a robot doing what God made me do."

John Calvin, a Swiss theologian, systematized the concept of predestination. He said: "There are infants in hell no bigger than the span of my hand." No sin was committed by them--they were in hell because they were born with Original Sin so, as sinners, could not be allowed to enter into heaven. He explained this to be the horrible backdrop against which the forgiveness of God could be understood and appreciated. To him, God predestined at the time He created the world those who would be saved and those who would go to hell.

There are vastly different ideas about what God is like. You need to open yourselves to understand God's love and have a logical answer to your faith.

Sorry, we got started in our discussion so soon that I did not introduce our visitor, Amanda. She's a high school student from Tacoma, Washington. She is visiting with her grandparents in Sacramento. I know you will welcome her, especially since she has just starting her journey of Christianity. You will have the challenge of sharing some of your own views with her.

You have a question, Amanda. Will you share it with the group?

"Thank you. I've heard only a little bit about Christianity and other religions, so I get confused about the number of Gods there might be. Could you discuss something about how many Gods there are?"

Certainly, Amanda. Our discussion next week is about gods.

HOW MANY GODS ARE THERE?

"Thou shalt have no other gods before me."
Exodus 20:3

Welcome back, Amanda. Since we are all interested in your question, why not begin by telling us something about your confusions?

"Well, in the first place, some Jehovah's Witnesses came to my door and left me their book, 'MANKIND'S SEARCH FOR GOD.' It is an interesting book, but stated that Hinduism has over 330 million gods, not just a mere 3 million as you told us last week. I'm not trying to be funny or anything, but it just goes to show how difficult it is to know who to believe, or what to believe."

Great, Amanda. That is what these discussions are all about, we're trying to discover truths. Do not be afraid to bring your questions. No one can ask a question which is too small to be recognized. If you ask a question too big for us to answer, we will be pleased to explore it with you. I guess the figure of 330 million was just too big for me to put in my memory bank.

There is a constant need to cross-check information and data. Even beliefs about religions which have been handed down through many generations need to be examined.

For instance, religions declared that the world was flat. Think about this: even scientists of that time also taught that the world was flat. Religion accepted what scientists believed to be true. Don't just blame religion for having too small a view.

Scientist are not necessarily atheists. It was Scientists who designed and built the pyramids of Egypt. They constructed the great wall of China; erected Babylon and graced it with hanging gardens, one of the seven wonders of the world; science worked out the plan to build the Roman aqueducts, bringing water from hills far away into cities with population explosions. Those feats still amaze us. The

scientists were religious people, some were so religious they worshipped many gods.

     "But do people of modern religions think about
having more than one God?" asked Jennifer. "Do the
people of India today still have all those millions
of gods?"

     "A thing that bothered me when I started going
to the Catholic Church was all the images and saints
I had to accept," Jesse commented. "I was taught to
differentiate between God the Father, God the Son,
and God the Holy Ghost. Mary is now glorified, it
seems that she became a fourth God in heaven. The
Catholic Church has existed from the time of Christ.
It claims to have authority to have the only truth
about Christianity. Are there, then, four Gods in
heaven?"

     Jesse, I appreciate this contribution you have
made to our discussion, but discussing the tenets of
faith of various religious bodies is a whole different type of ball-game, if you get my meaning.

     Maybe we can get at your question by going back
to Amanda's question, and take a historical perspective on the development of the idea of God.

     Since the very beginning of Man's ability to do
rational thinking, questions about the purposes and
future of life have been a central theme:

     "Who am I?"

     "Why am I here?"

     "Where did I come from?"

     "What is the meaning of life?"

     "What happens when I die?"

     "Is there a God who cares what happens to me?"

     "Do I have a choice, or must I just live out my
fate?"

     The struggle for answers has created many gods.
Every need or fear caused people to create a god who
would be in charge of that aspect of living. We had
this topic in a previous discussion, Amanda, but it
was necessary to touch on it again for your benefit.

     Do any of you remember the term to express both
animate and inanimate objects had spirits, that they
were gods?

     "Isn't that 'animism'?" Laura answered.

     Right on. You see, rather than being able to
communicate with God, primitive people had about the
74

same urge within them to worship as we do, so formed their own gods. Each individual made a unique god.

The Hindu people were quite imaginative. they were thirsty to understand the purpose of life and the universe. Through thousands of years there were millions of Hindus creating gods, so that comment about there being 330 million gods is probably true.

Not only did they create their earth gods, they contemplated about the Eternal Reality, the Creator of all things. Much of Hindu religious thinking ran parallel to Christianity and to religions which deal with an eternal supernatural Being.

Since I believe that God has been in communication with Man from the beginning, I think the phenomenon of different religions seeming to say the same things is not borrowing ideas from other people, but a reality of the spirit of God touching the lives of different people whenever or wherever they lived.

Amanda: "Do I understand that God is absolutely true and eternal? Wouldn't that mean that the words of God are always the same? I sure have heard a lot of different things about what God said."

"It is a hard thing to accept that God says the same thing to different people and in a wide span of time," David thought. "I have been studying about how those anthropologists, historians, theologians, biological scientists and archaeologists are busy at trying to link discoveries of today with origins in the past. They come up with some peculiar theories and data, but they don't always agree."

Strange, isn't it? Numerous scientists look to the past to find answers to the mysteries being seen today. It is almost as if they thought people once had more awareness of God than we do. There is the implication that God communicated more intimately to primitive people than with us; also, that God tells some people things not told to others. These sometimes conflict according to how people hear what God reveals to them.

Here is a quandary: are there so many gods telling so many different things to so many people that they create confusion in the religious thoughts of mankind?

Actually, it seems to me the problem of differing ideas about God is not in what God communicates

to man, but in how Man has received and interpreted
those communications.

How many of you have played the simple game of
"Telegraph"? It is where one person starts a statement by whispering it to the person next to him. It
is passed around the circle in the same manner. The
message can be whispered only once. Recipients must
pass on whatever message is understood, or misunderstood. The last person repeats aloud whatever message is received. I can not remember ever having been
in that game when the message ended the same way it
was started.

Isn't it possible that communications from God
have had the same problem?

You have also heard of witnesses to an accident
who do not agree. It is an accepted phenomenon that
no two people will have the same description of the
accident.

Religious beliefs had to be transmitted by word
of mouth before writing was invented. Some stories
were in pictures which now must be interpreted.

I saw interpreting being done with some ancient
Mayan hieroglyphics when I visited the ruins. There
were differing translations being read from the same
engraved pictures. It helped me understand how easy
religious beliefs can honestly be transmitted, but a
message being received may not be the same as it was
originally given.

God's eternal message is always the same. Man,
on the other hand, is not always the same. Man must
hear according to a myriad of conditions. Messages
heard are not always transmitted just as received.

Man's limited abilities to understand, and the
situations of living so varied that there eventuates
variations in the hearing of the transmitted message
from God. The Bible is, therefore, thought to have
many opposing meanings.

Of course there is progression. The astronauts
rise into space because of developments from yesterday's discoveries. Electronics is so innovative that
it generates new items so rapidly that about as soon
as you buy an item it is already antiquated. We are
told that every year's automobile is the product of
eight years of work in the designing stage. You buy
a car which manufacturers have already outdated.

We laughed as we hear that over a hundred years
ago the patent office decided it should be closed as
everything which could be invented had already been
invented.

The same thing is true with religion. Mankind
has only touched the fringe of the knowledge and the
love of God. The making of many gods expresses mankind's drive to be able to have a god no bigger than
our own understanding. "I don't know" is one of the
hardest things to admit.

Dogmatic religions tell you they know the whole
truth. We have admitted that some of the most harm-
ful and barbaric wars in all of history were fought
over religion. We want to be safe in our own sphere
of ideas. It is frightening for most people to ven-
ture into the unknown. It is threatening to our ego
to accept that other people's ideas may be true and
that our ideas may be wrong. It is disturbing to a
little child to be taken out of its play-pen and exposed to the vastness of the city's park.

It is hard for us to really accept the oneness
of God, and to grant that He is greater than we are.

When Moses was given the "Ten Commandments" he
came down from the mountain of inspiration and found
the people had already built for themselves a golden
calf to worship. God's First Commandment stated that
the Lord God was One God. The Israelites had been in
Egypt and remembered the glories and powers given to
those gods. An idol they could touch and take with
them seemed to offer more than this unseen God. They
wanted a god allowing them to enjoy drunkenness and
loose living. Release from slavery brought a desire
for absolute freedom and hilarious happinesses. They
did not understand that absolute freedom results in
chaos and un-Godliness.

Absolute religious freedom also leads to chaos
and anarchy, if you please. Such chaos and anarchy
leads to rebellion against religions by "thinkers."
Rejection of religion is atheism, humanism, trusting
in fate and astrological signs.

"I don't understand why 'thinkers' reject religion," Amanda commented.

Not all wise men reject God, but lots of confusion today comes from scholars who thought religions
did not fit into the new knowledge they had gained.

Self-protection and group acceptance are pressures toward the glorification of individuals, toward the status of free-thinkers and self-made individuals.

Another human tendency is to make God fit into our particular lives. We create images of God which fit into our concepts of what we want God to be. We may not agree with the ancient Hindu people, but the diversity of modern religions would seem to be quite similar. I wonder if some future religious history student will be saying that in American and European countries of the twentieth century there existed 330 million gods?

One of the explanations of the continuing identity of the Hebrew people is that they were selected by God to witness to monotheism--a belief that there is but one God. We discussed the "Ten Commandments" starting with the declaration: "The Lord your God is ONE GOD."

I see no logical reason to believe God divided Himself into many Gods. I see no logical reason to think that God is incapable of being where He wants to be, or doing whatever He desires to do. I can not imagine that God needed to create other Gods to take care of the universe and its creatures.

I do believe in God becoming special manifestations in order to demonstrate unique things for mankind. Those manifestations are not individual Gods, but the wonder of eternal God entering time, and the mystery of His spirit taking on an earthly form.

To me, there is comfort and joy in recognizing the oneness of God. Such recognition creates within us the ability to approach God without fear.

WHAT IS THE NATURE OF GOD?

"He that loveth not knoweth not God; for God is love."   1 John 4:8

Different religions have their own views about God. Even people who believe in monotheism can differ in their views of God, and those within the same belief have conflicting definitions about His nature and existence. Can you give some examples of God's nature you have heard?

The Lord is terrible.
The Lord is vengeful. Vengeance is mine, saith the Lord.
Fear the Lord. Fear of the Lord is the begin-- ning of wisdom.
The Lord is the avenger (I Thessalonians 4:6).
Let the earth fear the Lord; let inhabitants of the world stand in awe of Him (Ps.3:3). O fear the Lord, ye his saints (Ps. 34:9).
Loving kindness.
Longsuffering.
Compassionate.
Just.
O.K. That gives a pretty good idea of the various statements which are made about God's nature. Is that list satisfactory to you?

"Not me," Laura responded. "I don't like having God pictured as being fearful, jealous, vengeful, or angry. I would like to have a discussion about what the Bible might have meant by using those different attributes."

It may be hard to believe, but almost all the references to God's anger, etc. come out of the Old Testament.

Also, because we are not knowledgeable in other languages, we're not aware that some references have double meanings. Many of our modern words have new meanings which are opposite from traditional usages, such as: "Wow, that's bad, man," but it means something is good. Even the word "man" does not always mean the male gender. Haven't you heard women say:

"Man, that is a hard job"? "Far out" is not referring to something far away, rather, it has to do with
something which is admired or accepted.

When the Bible uses "awe" and "awesome," it is
expressing the reverence mankind should pay to God.
"Fear" of the Lord can also refer to paying respect
to God; it has about the same meaning as "honor." Of
course, there are times when actual terror is meant,
especially when evil is committed. The are numerous
passages within the Bible of God rejecting evil. Un-
il the time of Jesus, there was no way to atone for
ungodliness except by personal punishment.

Paul wrote about evil in Romans, as highlighted
in 6:23: "The wages of sin is death."

He admonishes us: "Be not deceived: God is not
mocked; whatsoever a man soweth, that shall he also
reap" (Galatians 6:7.

To a criminal, the law is terrible: something a
person fears. Laws are related to human crimes, but
sins relate to God. In Man's law a criminal may be
condemned or released by action of the law, but only
God can forgive sins. Since no one is perfect, the
people of the Old Testament often feared God. Their
fear was not from God being terrible, but because of
God's justice demanded atonements for evil deeds.
God never did require human sacrifices, but the
misunderstanding of Man brought about thinking that
a human-like God required nourishment from the life-
giving blood of humans, animals and birds. Also, it
was thought that God would be pleased with offerings
of precious gems, gold, silver, or fragrances. The
smoke of burnt offerings was thought to rise to God
and get His attention. Incense is still offered in
churches and temples around the world as token for a
sacrificial blessing.

The Old Testament has loving directions for Man
Moses revealed what he thought of God when he said:
"What doth the Lord require of you but to fear the
Lord thy God, to walk in all His ways, and to love
Him and to serve the Lord Thy God with all thy heart
and all thy soul" (Deuteronomy 10:12).

The prophet Micah repeats the same rejection of
sacrifices, but declares the Lord requires humility,
justice and loving mercy (Micah 6:6-8). He revealed
the concept of intimate relationships with God.
80

Does this sound like any of Jesus' admonitions?

Gayle had been in deep thought while listening: "That seems to be what Jesus answered when asked to name greatest commandment. He replied that the first and greatest commandment was in loving the Lord your God with all your heart, soul and mind; saying that the second was similar: 'loving your neighbor as you do yourself.' That's in Matthew 22:37-39."

Laura: "Isn't that the same thought Jesus gave when He compared the offerings of the rich man coming to the front of the temple and offering valuable gifts so they could be seen and honored, to the poor widow who stood in humility and offered only a mite, but offered it because she loved God. Jesus said her offering was more acceptable to God because she had shown her love rather than just to be seen of men.

"I've been bothered with that illustration because it appears to say that God doesn't appreciate the money we give to the church."

I see what you mean. The Old Testament, as well as the New Testament, repeatedly requires us to give a "tithe" to God's work. Have you come to a conclusion about the apparent difference?

"I guess the attitude of the heart toward God is the important thing. I think Jesus was pointing out that offerings are spiritually worthless unless they are given with the purpose of loving God with the gifts. But I know churches can use money which is given without any adoration of God. The money is blessed by being used in God's work, but that donor could not receive a spiritual blessing since he was only seeking to be honored by people."

That's the story of the rich couple who pretended to give all their wealth to the church, but kept half of it secretly for themselves, showing that the gift wasn't because they truly trusted themselves to the care of God. Their gift was not rejected by the church, but they fell dead because they attempted to fool God.

My interpretation of Ananias and Saphira (Acts 5:1-11) is that they became so stricken by their own guilt that they caused their own deaths. There's no place in that story which states that God took their lives. I am glad it is put that way because I do not see God as a killer. However, I would not be awfully

surprised if some of the people present then did not
praise God for those deaths. It is not unusual for
Man to blame God, or to give credit to God for something He had nothing to do with.

I heard a gambler praise God for his winnings,
then curse God for his loss. It didn't seem that God
had been involved with either action.

You see how our own inclinations or experiences
can formulate our image of the nature of God.

God is called, "Father." What kind of a nature
does that bring to your mind?

We constantly hear stories about the mother who
catches a child in a wrong then says, "Just you wait
until your father gets home! He'll punish you until
beg for mercy." What kind of God can this child see?

Consider the father who is too busy earning the
living to take time to outwardly demonstrate that he
loves his children. Would a child in this home know
about the intimate and caring love of God?

Mother spends her day cooking and cleaning and
running errands for the children and taking them to
the park or other places. "Mother" is not used as a
reference to God, however.

You have heard of the father who runs away from
his family, leaving them without a means of support.
The children wondered what was wrong with them which
caused their father to abandon them. A father like
this gets lots of publicity. Welfare rolls have many
"absent father" cases. Would a child in such homes
have an image of God who is dependable and helpful?

You have probably all heard of drunken fathers
who are unconcerned for their children, their wives
or their communities. They some times beat up their
wives or children, and cause fights among neighbors.
Can you imagine the image a "Father" God would have
to children with a father like this?

Practically every day you can read of battered
women, but who ever hears of battered fathers? The
father is so terrible that no one dares batter him!
God is so terrible, to some people, that they can't
see any reason to praise Him. Being afraid of God
can bring no joy into our lives.

"Do you mean that God can be seen in all those
images?" gasped Jennifer. "Doesn't the Bible openly
declare that God is love?"

82

Suppose you were a member of a family with the type of father just mentioned. You went to a church and heard God being referred to as Heavenly Father. What type of nature would you attribute to a Father-God? If the church gave you a picture of a God who was vicious and cruel, who abandoned you, etc., you would have some difficulty struggling to understand a loving God.

Our understanding of God's nature is limited to our experiences. We can intellectually study about God; we can listen to the testimonies of others; but we'll not actually know the love of God. God's love grows as a part of own consciousness, a part of our own experiences. Until then, we may intellectually know of God and be obedient to God's laws, but we'll not have His loving intimacy. Fear has no joy.

David: "I suppose you are going to tell us that the blind men who experienced the elephant differed in their ideas of the nature of Elephant? You said that what we touch can influence what we think about the total reality. We can not touch all of God, does that mean are we limited in our thinking about god?"

A slight clarification, David. If your "touch" means "to experience," you have stated a real truth.

Isn't the elephant tale logical? God could be seen as unmovable like a wall. He could be flexible like the ear. He could be hard and piercingly sharp like the tusk. Yet, like the story, none of the men could understand or accept the others' experiences.

Each of the blind men thought he knew what the whole elephant looked like--each of us accept from our own experiences what the nature of God is, but none of us know God from someone else's experience. However, if we make that experience our own, we may receive a substitutionary enrichment.

"That could be the meaning of the theme at our church's annual meeting this year: 'Listen With The Ears Of Your Heart.' I wasn't sure what it meant at the time, but I guess they were intending to get us to have more than just knowledge," Laura commented.

Gayle, "Was that what Revelations 2:7 meant by saying: 'He that hath ears to hear, let him hear'?"

There is a lot more to understanding than just what we hear with our ears. You have probably said something to a person, then found out that they had

not "heard" a word you said. One of the techniques
for counselors is "active listening." "Passive listening" is sitting in the presence of someone, with
your mind thinking of other things.

Thank you, Laura, for bringing the thought from
your annual meeting. We do need to be involved with
what we hear. We need Gayle's reference to keep us
alert to what we hear.

"But we hear a lot of useless trash. I find it
necessary to close my ears to a bunch of noises, at
work and around people," David protested.

Certainly there are good and bad things. It is
essential for us to be aware that we are constantly
needing to strain out valuables from useless things.
Some of you have heard me tell of my experience in
Manila, the Philippines, when a hurricane brought
hail. No Filipino had ever experienced hail. There
was no word in the Tagalog language to define it. If
people of Manila went to the island of Cebu to tell
about their experience, they wouldn't be understood
because neither had it ever hailed in Cebu.

Missionaries have the same kind of problem when
they try to explain God's love and salvation through
Jesus' death on the cross. Christianity sounds like
nonsense to people who worship terrifying idols. It
is not easy to bring them to   a loving God.

"There are some words describing God that I do
not understand," Jesse said. "Can we discuss some of
these? What do these words mean: 'omniscient,' 'omnipotent,' 'omnipotent,' and 'transcendent'? Words
like 'longsuffering,' 'imminent,' or 'infinite' are
more understandable."

These are simply theological terms; they say in
one word what we would say in several words. We can
understand them better if we list them on the board:

Omnipotent. This is taken from the Greek word
"omni" which means all-inclusive. You know the word
"potent" means strong or powerful. So, the meaning
of omnipotent would be, "all-powerful." That is used
to signify God is powerful enough to do anything. He
can move mountains, still the storms, create a star,
make time stand still.

Omniscient. Again the word starts with "omni."
"Scient" is the word from gives us the English word,
science. It also refers to knowledge or, wisdom.

84

That's right, David. Putting those Greek words together means that God is all-knowing. He knows a thought even before we think it; He understands the intricate mathematics of an Einstein; He knows exact measurements of the universe and the number of stars therein; He's so inter-meshed with you that he knows the number of hairs on your head.

<u>Imminent</u>. This word is used to denote that God is not isolated in some far distant "heaven," but is hovering among us. You have probable heard the word used to express "imminent danger," something that is capable of happening immediately. It is the essence of our discussion about "God is here."

<u>Transcendent</u>. Briefly, this means that God is more than human: He is defined as being beyond, being greater, being superior. When we state that God transcends time and space, you see, we are expressing His eternality and limitlessness.

<u>Infinite</u>. This means that God is unlimited. It can refer to anything: love, knowledge, patience and any other attribute.

<u>Longsuffering</u>. The questions such as: "When is God going to erase evil, hunger, pain and inhumanity of Man?" are answered in this concept. God is aware of our natures and is very tolerant of our mistakes. This does not imply that God likes our mistakes, but it is stating that God gives us time to work through our problems without His immediate condemnation and punishment.

The thirteenth chapter of First Corinthians is Paul's statement of love. Modern translations make the archaic word "charity" into the more significant word "love." Remember, God is love. Only God could perfectly fulfill the conditions of this passage.

<u>Omnipresent</u>. This one is easier now, isn't it? Jennifer tells us that it means God everywhere. Not only with us, but present in the entire universe.

We have discussed the first beliefs concerning the presence God isolated Him confined to a specific locality. Religion taught that the earth was flat, and science agreed. Then science made the discovery that the world was round, and the center of the universe. Today, we stand in amazement at such a giant cosmos, having no real concept of its magnitude nor of its nature.

Keep in mind the fact that God is the same yesterday, today, and forever. We are the ones who make changes, but from our stationary viewpoint, the universe appears to change. Although motionless (?), the stars seem to revolve around us, just like they did thousands of years ago.

God's eternal nature is love. Love can desire only good for loved-ones. Love yearns for a loving response.

Human experiences tend to reject those who deny us, and to be friends with those who are friendly to us. Even when we love someone and find rejection by that person our loves may cease to be expressed, but they do not die.

We were created with the nature of God. If we draw near to God, He will draw near to us. God lives with us, but if we turn away from Him we will not be to benefit by His presence. He will always hold out His inviting arms, but we will be unable to respond to His invitation. We may even say: "God is dead."

"It is not the will of God that any should perish" (2 Peter 3:9).

Matthew:23:37 tells that Jesus yearned over the city of Jerusalem, but it would not respond. He wept as He cried out: "O Jerusalem, Jerusalem, how often would I have gathered thy children about me even as a hen gathers her chickens under her wing, but you would not!"

The purpose of God is declared in John 3:16,17. You've quoted those verses: "God so loved the world that He sent His only begotten Son into the world that whosoever believes on Him should not perish but have everlasting life. For God sent not His Son into the world to condemn the world but that the world through Him might be saved."

There is no other religion which provides this type of salvation. Other religions have do-it-yourself systems, but none offer the forgiving love of God as a gift. Accepting a gift is an experience.

GOD CALLS US TO EXPERIENCE HIS LOVE WITHOUT FEAR.

DID GOD CREATE EVIL?

"I make peace, and create evil: I the Lord do all these things."

Isaiah 45:7

"You can not make me believe God created evil," Laura protested.

"Satan is the evil one," Gayle offered. "He is the cause of all evil."

David, "Then we must ask where Satan came from. Are there two eternal Beings contending forever with each other?"

Are we in deep trouble tonight? Should we fear such a question? We could ignore it? It is strange that no one asked Jesus to answer this question. Do you think He did not want to answer it and made it impossible for people to ask where evil came from? What was the purpose of Jesus?

A chorus of voices answered: "For God so loved the world that He sent His only begotten Son into the world that whosoever believeth on Him should not perish but have everlasting life."

Does that give us a basis for understanding why no one asked Jesus about where evil came from? Evil was so prevalent in the world, and had been such an accepted condition of both the religious and social realms that no one considered asking about where it came from. It just was always there!

That does not answer our question, does it? God declared through Isaiah that He created evil.

What did He mean?

One of the agonizing courses in seminary was a discussion of evil. Theologians have struggled with the question of evil throughout many centuries. It is in the mind of every person who asks, "How could God let it happen?" "Why doesn't God do something?" It is implied in the question, "Why does God permit evil people to prosper?" You call evil most every-thing which happens to us: sickness, poverty, crime, destructive forces of nature, unlovely relationships and contentious children. We put the blame on God!

We even ask: "Why did God allow Adam and Eve to disobey Him by listening to the serpent, then eating the forbidden fruit?" The serpent, Satan, seems to have had legs then. As punishment for enticing Adam and Eve to sin, the Lord made the snake to crawl on its belly; its skeleton still shows legs.

Can we ask such questions? Would we imply that God didn't know what He was doing? Are we suggesting that God made a mistake? Should evil never have been allowed in the first place? In a way, wouldn't we be saying that we know more than God about how the universe should have been created and operated?

"You're hurting my brains," protested Jennifer. "I thought we were coming here for a simple answer, but now I am getting more confused than ever."

Confusion is part of every solution. We would ask no questions if we never became confused. We'd be like mere babies sitting all day long sucking our thumbs in mindless acceptance of things as they are.

Life is an exciting experience. It is full of changes and needs to constantly overcome obstacles. We drive our cars, but we know that we must stop for repairs and gas. Why don't we inquire: "How do manufacturers get away with building cars that forever need repairing, and are always running out of gas?"

Two answers come out of our discussion tonight, Jennifer.

First, the historic answer: there are two eternal Beings. One God is good, the other is evil. As we have discussed already, co-existence in eternity would mean that neither was "born," neither could they ever "die."

Second, there is but one God who created everything. Tonight's Scripture says God created evil.

The first answer declares that just as there is light and darkness, so there is good and evil. That is the way things are and always have been. It says that there is an eternal warfare going on. Satan is constantly endeavoring to overthrow God, and God is constantly contending to eliminate evil. Thus, we're in the fall-out of that battle. Mankind is the prize each side struggles for; we are powerless; we aren't participants in that war; we are "fated" to be the results of that eternal conflict. Fate cries: "Sera, sera! Whatever will be will be"!

88

Free-will says you may choose to be part of the family of God, or choose to be a slave to Satan.

Back to your pain, Jennifer. I can not believe that God's intentions for you is that you are merely a pawn in a celestial chess game. God loves you; He cares about you. In order for you to be yourself, it is necessary to have the opportunity to rebel. It is also necessary to have the freedom to choose to love God. You could not make such a choice if God merely created you in the Garden of Eden with no chance for making a choice. All temptations come from the presence of evil, which must always appear wonderful. It is necessary, therefore, to be constantly alert and to know the difference. Jesus came to show The Way, and to give us the strength to walk therein.

Jesse had a twinkle in his eyes as he said, "If evil is so enticing, and being good is the opposite of evil, then being good must be very unexciting."

Remember our discussion of the bacchanalias of ancient Rome? They actually believed that there was no heaven to gain and no hell to shun. Their highest good, therefore, was to indulge in the greatest possible pleasures. Bacchanalias, you know, were orgies of drunkenness and unlimited lovemaking. The god of wine and revelry, Bacchus, was their god.

Dionysus, the Greek counterpart, was god of the Neo-Epicureans who taught, "Eat, drink and be merry, for tomorrow you may die."

Enticing as evil may be, it lives only until it destroys its worshippers. Evil is like the bait in a trap which seems desirable, but leads to death.

Most Hindu sects teach austerity in order to be free from evil. Would you believe they teach sex to be the greatest evil? Buddha taught that sex was so great a pleasure it would lead to the abandonment of striving toward spiritual enlightenment. Other evil includes money, sickness, politics, war and vanity.

One of the early explanations of the origin of evil given to me was of the wood shavings. In order to create a piece of furniture, it was necessary to discard sawdust, shavings and scraps of wood. Every item worked on created scraps. Evil was the residue resulting from producing that which was good.

Have you gone fishing with lures and flies? As a fisherman, you do everything possible to make the lure enticing. The unsuspecting fish bites at the lure and is caught. Death to the fish!

I repeat, evil is enticing, even exciting, but it is deadly to the soul. Evil always separates you from God. It may not eternally condemn you, however. That is where God's love comes in.

Here is a little poem attributed to Vishnu, the Hindu supreme god, when he appeared as Krishna:

Cling to me!
Clasp me with your heart and mind!
So shall you dwell with me on high;
If you are so weak as to set
Body and soul upon me constantly,
Despair not.
Give me the lower services!
Seek to know me,
Worship with a steadfast will;
And, if you cannot worship constantly,
work for me the works pleasing to me!
For he who labors out of love for me
Shall finally attain!
But, if in this your faint heart also fails,
Bring me your failures! Find refuge in me."

Krishna was not discussing the origin of evil; he knew it existed. He knew all humans experienced it. He does not demand perfection, only that people turn their hearts and minds toward him. He does not offer salvation, only refuge.

I have recommended many times that the book of Job should be read as a treatise on evil. It starts out with a discussion between Satan and God. (Satan, Lucifer, had already been cast out of heaven, so God asked him where he came from.) Satan is permitted to test Job to see if this righteous man could be induced to deny God. Satan must not kill Job, however.

Job's family was taken away; he was deprived of his wealth; he was given horrible skin sores and put into a pit of ashes. There his friends came accusing him of sinning, but he continued declaring the glory of God. "Curse God, and die!" they advised, but Job would only praise God.

Satan did everything he could to make Job angry enough to deny God, but Job resisted everything.

Finally, God appears before Job and reminds him that although he was a good man, he had not created

90

the universe. Job was so proud of his righteousness that God had to reveal that he needed to be humble.

Righteousness was Job's sin. He humbled himself before God and was healed. His property and family were restored to him.

Where did evil come from? Evil was not evident at first because Job was complacently wealthy and at peace with God and the world.

God did not call that evil, however. When evil was thrown at Job by Satan, Job remained faithful to God. Satan made him suffer so he would deny God.

Galatians 6:10-16 is Paul's encouragement when faced with troubles such as Job had.

Jesse recites: "Finally, my brethren, be strong in the Lord, and in the power of His might. Put on the whole armor of God, that ye may be able to stand against the wiles of the devil. For we wrestle not against flesh and blood, but against principalities, against powers, against the rulers of the darkness of this world, against spiritual wickedness in high places. Wherefore take unto you the whole armor of God, that ye may be able to withstand in the evil day, and having done all, to stand. Stand, therefore, having your loins girt about with truth, and having on the breastplate of righteousness; and your feet shod by the preparation of the gospel of peace; above all, taking the shield of faith, wherewith ye shall be able to quench all the fiery darts of the wicked. And take the helmet of salvation, and the sword of the Spirit, which is the word of God. Praying always with all prayer and supplication in the Spirit, and watching thereunto with all perseverance and supplication for all saints."

Thank you, Jesse. That passage sends shivers of reverence down my spine. Did it mean anything to the rest of you?

Paul wasn't involved with the question of where evil came from. His aim was to assist the Galatians in knowing how they could withstand the its constant rain of bombardments.

What was that, David? You asked about where Satan came from? If you believe in the eternal duality of God and Satan, your question will be meaningless because there is no beginning with eternity. Nothing is "from" anywhere when there is no beginning.

If you consider God's statement that He created evil, your answer is that Satan was created by God.

Many years ago I fantasized about Satan with a scenario. I took some Bible passages, did some philosophizing, used a little logic, and built a scenario which goes like this:

"In the beginning God created the heavens and the earth. The emptiness could not fulfill the need of God to have loving companionship, so the heavenly angels were created. One of the angels was Lucifer (Satan). Lucifer was given a special place as leader of the angels, and the freedom to respond to God's love. He was brilliant: he shined like the morning star. Lucifer began to be so proud of his position that he attempted to be greater than God. An angel is everlasting, so God cast Lucifer and his followers down to earth. Satan continued to try to become the supreme ruler of the universe.

"God created humans to populate the earth. He breathed into mankind His holy spirit and gave mankind living souls. Satan was not satisfied to rule only his angels, he began the great struggle to capture everything God had created. Satan promoted his rebellion against God--promoted sin. Having created Satan, God had to admit that He created sin."

This has been a lengthy session, but we have a question yet to be answered: "Will the struggle ever come to an end?"

Yes. Satan will be destroyed! The where, when and how may not be clear, but it will surely happen. God, the Creator, is also the final Judge. Evil can never again get into heaven.

The Bible says that Satan will be bound a thousand years, then released. It seems to me that what we are being shown is that Satan will be cleansed of his evil, along with all his followers. The end of time will result in everything being returned to the sinlessness of God's eternal love.

On a church bulletin board was the following:

> God is not permissive.
>
> If He were, we would have
>
> "The Ten Suggestions."

As we have said: "God's perfect love cannot be tainted by the presence of evil." Evil, therefore, can never be admitted into eternity.

IS GOD A MAN OR A WOMAN?

"There is neither male nor female"
Galatians 3:28

The apostle Paul had struggles with beliefs of paganism and other religions: he had to demonstrate the differences between the teachings of Jesus and the destructiveness of worshipping human-like gods.

Paul emphasized the spiritual reality of faith as differing from pagan practices. He wrote Galatians to speak into a culture which worshipped many gods, both male and female. We discussed something of this when we spoke of the Greek concept of "heaven" as being on Mt. Olympus where gods resided. They got involved with earth-bound human lovers and had demi-god children who became the Greek heroes. They had physical contests, became angry with each other and with humans; they played with human life just as a child might play with toy soldiers.

Paul taught that God is ONE. Which of the gods would He resemble? The Corinthians worshipped Aphrodite, the goddess of fertility. Women went into the temple of Aphrodite to worship by participating in fertility rites (sex). I am not sure that the men saw this as an act of worship! There was no sense of real love in the sexual activities of the temple.

When Paul addressed the Christians in Corinth, he laid down a strict law that women were to remain covered, and must not teach in the church. He demanded complete separation from the Aphrodite practices so Christian worship would not resemble paganism.

It is hard to erase generations of old beliefs. Aphrodite, the epitome of sexuality, had been in the minds of the people of Corinth for many hundreds of years. Their God was a woman. I do not think it was the woman-god which Paul was troubled about, but the holiness and purity of both men and women within the Christian fellowship, and in marriage.

Ancient Hinduism had many female gods. There were probably more male gods. If you were to consolidate all the millions of Hindu gods into ONE, what would that ONE be--male or female?

Making God out of our own images produces both male and female figures, as well as having God take on the characteristics of every ethnic group.

God might be pictured as an African pygmy or an Australian aborigine. He might resemble the Chinese or an Englishman. He has been depicted in shades of black, yellow, brown and red. All races seem to want to have God be a mirror-image of themselves.

During the span of time in which the Bible was written, men ruled. God, therefore, was represented as a man. Not only that, but there is no inclusive pronoun in English to express God without the gender of male or female. We are compelled to use the non-generic "He." Good grammar teaches that "it" may be used only for non-humans or inorganic matter. There is the possibility of using the third person pronoun "they" to express even single entities, but it would hardly be correct grammar in reference to the spirit of God's unique oneness, would it?

Today's efforts to say, "God, she," shows that the urge to humanize God is still with us. There is even a publication of the Bible which takes out all "sexist" language. Jesus is titled: "Child of God." All references to "Father" become "The Almighty," or some other non-sexist word. There is no "boy" in the life of Jesus. He did not become "a man." Jesus did not ascend unto "His" "Father."

It's interesting that the Sadducees, who denied any resurrection, asked Jesus what would happen to a woman who successively married seven brothers after each one died. Which would be her husband in heaven?

I am sure that Jesus saw this question as nothing more than heckling, but He gave a direct answer: "In the resurrection they neither marry nor are given in marriage, but all are one as the angels of God in heaven" (Mt. 22:38).

Note the way Jesus began His answer: "You err, not knowing the Scriptures, nor the power of God."

"I am not sure that I like that description of heaven," Gayle protested. "I have always been told that when we get into heaven we will rejoin our families. What joy would there be in heaven for me if I were not allowed to be with my loved ones?"

That's really a tough question, Gayle. Finding the answer has divided Christianity ever since theologians (or first Christians) asked the question two thousand years ago.

Do you have your Bibles open to Matthew 22? Can you imagine what the Sadducees believed about life after death? Let us take a moment to reflect on what Jesus meant when He said "resurrection."

What do you think, Jesse?

"Well, the Sadducee could not have been talking about Jesus' resurrection; that hadn't happened yet. Neither could the Scribes have understood what Jesus came into the world to accomplish. I am not certain what that passage meant."

You are partly right, Jesse. Does anyone else want to help with our understanding?

Laura, "Does that have anything to do with the apostle Paul's statement before the Roman governor? Paul said the Jews accused him of being disobedient to the Roman god-emperor, Caesar, but that the real question was on the resurrection at the day of judgment (Acts 24:15). The Jews were vehemently opposed to Paul. Could a Roman comprehend the issue?"

Why do you think there was such intense anger against Paul?

David's research for his term paper had led him to the division in Hebrew theology: "It seems to me that the Sadducees and Pharisees were having different conclusions about the resurrection from what the priests and Levites believed," he reported. "There was the argument about whether it was only those who were properly sanctified, or would everyone receive the resurrection? Paul preached that all who accepted Jesus Christ would receive Christ's resurrection without regard to a Hebrew religious relationship. "That doctrine sent both sides into a wild frenzy!"

Hebrew religion was obedience to the Law. While no firm picture of eternity was in evidence, it was believed that those keeping the Law would be justified in the resurrection, but those who's names were not written in the "Book of Life" would be in Sheol. There was a very physical image "after the resurrection." After all, their God lived in the firmament.

The Law did not allow a man to marry two wives. The Sadducee had a perfectly logical legal question, but Jesus was not about to be caught in their trap. They were the lawyers of the day, so were interested in posing legal interpretive questions. When a woman married and her husband died, she had the legal duty to marry his brother and have an heir in the family, but all seven died without conceiving a child, so a natural question would be: "Whose wife would she become when they all got to heaven?"

This is similar to your question, Gayle. It is the same question that millions of people ask. Those Sadducees and Priests had their own answers, but not agreements. Christianity has been divided with such doctrinal interpretations.

Questions:

1. "Will I have physical family relationships in heaven?"

2. "Will I have some humanly form when I get up there in heaven?"

Remember what I said I was taught when about as old as you are? That church taught that heaven was paved with gold; that there were great mansions and little huts reserved for whatever glory you had laid up for yourself. I expected to go through a pearly gate; I would be given a harp to play on throughout eternity; I would wear a golden crown which would be studded with the stars and precious jewels I earned by my attendance at Sunday School or church; I would be taken before the great white throne on which God sat with Jesus at His right hand and the Holy Spirit on His left. I worked hard to get awards so I could be given the beautiful mansion prepared for me.

I didn't feel that there was anything illogical in that conception then. It said that I was to live in "my" house. That was O.K. At that time I was not thinking of living in relationship with my family.

You know that I like to joke about things. As I thought some more about the picture of heaven, I did the terrible thing of joking about it. I asked about how I was to find the homes of the other members of my family, and whether I would have to live alone in my mansion. I asked if I would be my own cook and if I would have to do my own housekeeping, since this would not be the home of my parents. I wondered if I could expect to have someone live with me.

My pastor was a very serious person. He did not like the way I joked about heaven. My teachers also did not like my asking serious questions that were

beyond what they had already believed to be absolute
truths.

I was taught that eternity was headed by three
MEN. These men agreed together, and were called "the
God-Head." I was told that just as an egg is a yolk,
a shell, and an albumin (the white), "God" also is a
trinity made up of the Father, the Son, and the Holy
Ghost.

The more I studied the Bible, the more confused
I became about the actuality of God. The more study
I made of the reality and magnitude of the universe,
the more it seemed unlikely that God was a physical
figure and be covering all the vast universe at the
same time. I could not even understand that He was
everywhere around this planet at the same time.

I read Darwin's "Origin of the Species." It had
some logical observations, but where was God in that
idea? Is accidental evolution the ultimate answer of
life and the world? Am I only an accident which came
out of a meaningless speck of dust?

Studies of religions around the world convinced
me that there was something within each of us which
responded to an ultimate direction. Victor Frankl, a
German-Jew psychologist who became famous after his
release from a concentration camp during the second
World War, composed a book entitled MAN'S SEARCH FOR
MEANING in which he called this in-dwelling mystery,
"The unconscious God." He did not mean that God was
unconscious, but that God dwells in our unconscious
minds, and His pervasive presence is speaking to our
sub-conscious level, constantly endeavoring to rise
into our consciousness. He is in every person, just
like He always has been and always will be. Frankl
wrote of God's presence as love. Man's ultimate end
and purpose, as revealed in the light of God, therefore, is to love God and to love one another.

What is love? What did it mean that "God is a
spirit"? What was Paul meaning when he said that we
would be changed? What did he mean when he said the
corruptible could not inherit incorruption? He wrote
that when we get to heaven we will not have earthly
bodies.

There is only one conclusion I draw from this:

GOD IS NOT MALE!

It no longer disturbed me to hear of the Bible as only drawing glorious pictures for me. Now I was convinced that eternity's reality was much greater than I could possibly understand in this life. I no longer had to believe that what I thought was what all persons had to accept as the ultimate truth.

Accepting God as being Love, I came to realize that Love is the spirit. It is a dimension different from physical relationships.

I began my adventuring into the nature of God, into His immensity. I could also accept that I was made in His image--but God's "image" is my spirit, my "soul," not my physical body.

Likewise, I drew a similar logical conclusion:

GOD IS NOT FEMALE.

Therefore, when I consider who I shall be when I go into the resurrection, my answer has to be, "I do not know!"

Since I do not see God as a physical being in a physical heaven, I expect that whatever I experience then will make me amazed at the expansiveness of the reality "up there." Love knows no boundaries.

I will not expect to see my aged mother too ill to hold my children in her arms, the mystery is that she will be changed. My friends will not be vigorous teenagers, nor decrepit old wrecks.

This is what I have grown to believe: we shall know each other by our personalities--by our loves.

In a like manner, God will know us through His spirit--through His love. God will not be male, nor will He be female. He is the spirit of eternal love.

It is only when we clone God from our physical bodies that we get into trouble. It is confusingly easy to fantasize heaven as being like some glorious place on earth--a paradise. Recall, however, God was existing before there ever was an earth. He needed no earthly abode. He will be existing when there is no more earth--no more universe. God is an eternal "esence" which needs no physical attribute such as size, gender, color or age.

DOES GOD HATE US AND DESTROY US?

"The wages of sin is death."
Romans 6:23

You began these discussions by stating that you were afraid of God, Jennifer. Did you want to start out by telling something about why you were fearful of Him?

"I think I have been afraid of God all my life. When I was a little child I was told that God would punish me if I did not obey. As I grew older, I did things which pleased me, but did not follow the laws I had been given," Jennifer answered. "Every time I didn't go into church I was afraid the of the Devil getting me and that God would punish me. My parents were very strict, but I did not always obey them. I could not picture my parents as ever being young and happy. I guess that made God seem to be strict and condemning. I did not know about God's love."

Are you saying now that a loving God should not punish you? The Bible is full of references to God's punishments.

"I know that now," she continued. "I've helped train horses and had to restrict them. I understand now that this may have seemed as punishment to them. They might have thought I hated them, but it was because I loved them that I struggled as I taught them how to behave.

"I can understand that a loving God must set up laws which would be intended to teach me how to live a good life, but I was afraid of God because He knew that I had broken His Laws and would punish me."

"How about the flood?" David asked. "The Bible says that God caused the flood. Doesn't that show a God who was angry and destroyed the people?"

That is not a trick question, is it? I'm happy with the way you are all asking questions, and some questions which seem to be unanswerable. Should God hate the people in the days of Noah?

While we are at it, let's include the cities of Sodom and Gomorrah which were also destroyed. These

cities are mentioned in the 19th chapter of Genesis.
The flood story is found in Genesis, chapters 6-10.

God also called out Jonah to tell a city named
Nineveh it was to be destroyed because of its wickedness. The story is in the book of Jonah, near the
end of the Old Testament

Here are three different locations, the cities
were many years apart. What did these have in common
besides being destroyed? Understanding these cities
could help us understand why they were destroyed.

David: "Each of those occasions begins with the
description of people being evil. They had departed
from God. They were enjoying selfish pleasures with
no regard for the welfare of the community. Nineveh
was not destroyed, however."

Wasn't it? Jonah did not recognize how much he
had succeeded. We certainly see him crying on a hill
overlooking the city and protesting against God for
not being faithful to His promise to destroy Nineveh
and its people. He did not consider God's viewpoint,
all he waited for was the evil city to be destroyed.

Jonah preached about its destruction. The city
repented and turned to God. The wicked city was destroyed! Jonah had caused its destruction, but was
too blinded by his own image of what would be done.
He sat there on the hillside in anticipation of the
fireworks and explosions he would enjoy as the city
was destroyed. Jonah showed no understanding of the
salvation to the thousands of people he had been in-
strumental in bringing back to God.

God is love. Wickedness has no place in God's
presence. These two stories were not about people as
individuals, but about unrestrained selfishness and
ungodliness. Evil was becoming so entrenched in the
lives of those people that there was no possible way
to change them. In order for loving people to have a
chance to develop, evil had to be eradicated. A new
opportunity had to be established.

About fifty years ago I was given John Calvin's
tremendous books about Christianity, "Institutes of
the Christian Religion." There were many passages in
that writing which shocked me, but the one I recall
vividly through is this: "We assert, that by eternal
and immutable counsel, God has once for all determined, both whom He would admit to salvation, and whom

100

He would condemn to destruction." He explained it
this way: "We affirm that this counsel, as far as it
concerns the elect, is founded on His gracious mercy
totally irrespective of human merit; but that those
to whom He devotes to condemnation, the gate of life
is closed by a just and irreprehensible, but incomprehensible, judgment" (Calvin liked big words). He
did not view predestination as anger or hate, but a
simple design of creation. I suppose it can be compared to building a house: the resulting trash must
be thrown away. The one who built the house did not
have feelings about the trash, it was just material
which resulted in shaping, cutting and plastering.
    God was the contractor building a the universe.
    Calvin saw sin in the world and had to come up
with an explanation. He distinguished "sheep" from
the "goats." Goats, a distinct species, can't change
themselves into sheep. Sinners could not be changed
into saints. No one had choices, nor should priests
try to save sinners whom God had designated to hell.
    Gayle, "But why didn't God just make everyone
to be admitted into salvation?"
    I was only explaining Calvin's view of predes-
tination. There was another theologian from Holland,
Jacobus Arminius, who declared that Calvin had been
in error. He taught that God is love; that love had
to be free to respond to another love. Therefore, he
said, God created mankind with free-will.
    Freedom involves the opportunity and the obli-
gation to make choices. Each individual must have a
free choice to love and do good, or to choose to do
evil and be selfish. God's gift of freedom demands
that He does not interfere--that we must ask Him to
help.
    Predestination answers the problem of evil by
placing its existence as the will of God.
    Free-will declares God must allow for evil, but
that it is not His will that any should choose to be
evil and perish. We read John 3:16 again "For God so
loved the world that He sent His only begotten Son
into the world, that whosoever believeth on Him
should not perish but have everlasting life."
    While I was in the Philippines, I learned this
phrase: "Ikaw ang masusinod" (probably wrong spell-
ing!) which translates to, "It's up to you."

Free-will seems to say the same thing: that God gives us all kinds of potentials, including a potential to become evil and be condemned, or to believe in Jesus and have everlasting life. It is up to you!

Paul's complete verse from Romans 6:23 is: "The wages of sin is death, but the gift of God is eternal life through Jesus Christ our Lord."

Jesse, "How about God acting in such a way that He would be different from His normal nature? Could it not be possible for God to hate us?"

I have been waiting a long time for just such a question, Jesse. Let us consider some of the things God cannot do. Yes, I am saying God has His limits.

First, God cannot refuse to be other than ultimate love. His love can never change. God is self-limiting. He can not rebel against His own love.

Second, God is not whimsical. We started these discussions by proposing that God is logical and is consistent. We can depend upon Him.

However, if God requires us to do something and promises blessings for our obedience, He also gives the other side of the promise--to punish when we are not obedient. Inconsistency would be if God allowed us to "get away with it" and reward us even when we have not been obedient. Could we trust in God if He changed His mind? Some people would even cheat!

Third, God's heaven is not a democracy.

Social customs and mores depend upon majority rule, but God sets absolute rules for living with righteousness. Those rules are always based on His love and our living with that love.

Fourth, God cannot manipulate us. Manipulation would make us no more than robots without a will of our own. Jesus could not manipulate the people when He lived on earth.

As we saw earlier, Jesus wept over the city of Jerusalem. He cried: "O Jerusalem, Jerusalem. How I wanted to draw you to me as a hen gathers her chickens, but you would not." Why didn't Jesus just pass his hand over Jerusalem and save everyone? He could not! He could not manipulate Man and remove him from his God-given freedom.

Fifth, God's absolutes cannot be changed. Pure love makes it impossible to become Satanic. God can not change from pure love. Love can suffer as well as rejoice, however. Jesus set the example for us so that we could understand that there may be "tears in the eyes of God." You recognize I have written that in quotation marks because it is a figure of speech, not a physical reality.

No, God cannot hate us. He must reject our sin, however.

God's apparent punishments are corrections for our faults. Galatians 6:7 puts it this way: "Be not deceived, God is not mocked, for whatsoever a man soweth, that will he also reap."

There are references in the Bible about a "Book of Life." These give a picture of the day of resurrection when the Book of Life will be opened and every person's good deeds will be balanced by evil deeds. This is an Old Testament picture carried over to the New Testament, but you must not miss how Christ's atonement changes it.

There are many Christians today who are frightened by what the Book of Life may balance out to be. They've read, "Work out your own salvation with fear and trembling" (Philippians 2:12).

The book of Isaiah (1:2) prophesied the Messiah as it says: "Tho your sins be as scarlet, they shall be washed white as snow." The Book of Life can have no fear for those who accept Jesus because He washes away their sins.

Experience forgiveness and you will understand the absolute love of God

"How can you get that experience?" Jesse asked.

"Sure, now we are back to not being able to be given experiences through other people." David went on. "It seems to me that we are contradicting what we said about having to experience God. How can we know about God without another person to help us?"

Laura, "Aren't there methods, meditations, ways of knowing how to get an experience or directions to drawing close to God?"

Jennifer was about ready to cry, but she asked, "Am I saved? I told you that I have been terrified most of my life, but I don't want to be in fear for the rest of my life. Can I know that I'm forgiven?"

Let's go back to the statement about God being not willing that any should perish. Wouldn't it be logical to believe that God must have made a way for us to not only be saved, but have a firm conviction that we are forgiven and have become members of His heavenly family.

We cannot get assurance from our own struggles. Nothing we can do, no actions, no works of charity, no sufferings or routine periods of worship or meditations will attain salvation for us.

"Faith" is a word most used to express knowing God. "Belief" is accepting something without having it documented by science. "Let go, and let God," is applicable to many situations; but mostly, it is God lovingly calling us to peace.

It is easy to say, "Accept Jesus Christ and you will be saved," but what does that mean?

Nothing in the Bible tells you to save yourself by your own strengths. Jesus came for that very purpose: to provide salvation for you. Now, you need to recognize the value of Jesus' free gift and receive it freely in order to have it. Accepting Christ is the experience of responding to His love and feeling His love come into your heart.

Doubt draws you away from God. Your experiences of love bring you ever closer to Him.

DOES GOD CARE WHAT HAPPENS TO US?

"Cast your cares upon Him, for He cares for you."
1 Peter 5:7

Now we come to the questions which begin, "Why doesn't God do something about...?"

We came pretty close to answering this query in our last discussion. We need to go a bit farther in this discussion because some of you were expressing concerns about God being far off from us and leaving us to our own devices.

"I don't agree with that. We have said that God is present with us when we talked about mystical experiences." Gayle remarked.

Why don't you tell us what you are remembering about that discussion, Gayle.

"We found that mystical experiences can be made to appear to be just accidents, hallucinations, and self-induced fantasies. The thrill of any mystical experience can be destroyed if we analyze it trying to prove what happened," Gayle answered.

From the intensity of your reply, I am sure you are remembering the rejections your friends made of your own intimate experience.

Here is a dramatic scenario of tonight's topic from Elijah's encounter with the priests of Baal. He had a contest with them to find whose God was effective. The priests were invited to be first to find if their god could consume the offering. A prolonged ceremony went on all day; they struggled and shouted and mutilated themselves to get Baal's attention; it did no good: there was no response. Elijah seems to have been having a joyous time as he taunted them to shout louder, offer more of their blood, dance with more zeal. Near evening, Elijah urged them to shout even louder; perhaps their god was sleeping and must be aroused; maybe their god was on a trip and had to have time to get back to them.

Then Elijah, with only a short time before the evening ritual of sacrifice, bowed briefly in front of the altar of stones the people had built for him, prepared a young bullock, laid it upon the altar and then had the people pour water over everything. The water flooded over the altar three times. There was no mistake about a trick, nor even a possibility for Elijah himself to kindle the fire needed to consume that water-soaked mess. He prayed to God, and a fire came down from heaven, consuming not only the offering, but all the wood upon the altar and the stones of the altar. Everything was consumed, including the water surrounding the altar! (1 Kings 18:17-38).

God made a dramatic demonstration: He cared.

David, the Psalmist, concluded: "The Lord shall neither slumber nor sleep" (Ps. 121:4).

In Jeremiah 41:10 the Lord says: "Fear not, be not dismayed, I am with you."

Jesus' response to whether God would be present is found in Matt. 28:20 where He promises: "Lo, I am with you always, even unto the end of the world."

Laura, "Those verses seem to support what we've talked about before, that God is just as real as you allow Him to be to you."

Yes. and if you are not dogmatic, your concept of God is always expanding. God remains infinite.

How expansive will you let God be to you? When I was hiking, I used to imagine climbing to the very top of all mountains. Mountain peaks revealed there was such an astounding number of mountains out there that I could never climb them all. I was awed by an awareness of their magnificence.

I did not have to climb every mountain, just as I do not need to know everything about God. Each of those peaks increased my reverential awe, just like each of our mountain-top experiences increases our awareness of the presence of God.

The growing wave of Hindu practices in America indicates the weakness of Christian beliefs. Mystic teachers entice you to gain perfection and be freed from the fate of reincarnated suffering. They offer no God to help you. None of the 330 million gods of India can help. Transcendental meditations may help calm your troubled soul, but can't forgive you. You carry your self-made god around with you, but you're the only source of its power.

Psychological self-motivations are often based in atheism; they're unable to call upon God's wisdom
106

or power. Creating ourselves into our own deity can result in denying the reality of God.

Three of the Gospels included Jesus' statement: "I came not to call the righteous, but the sinners to repentance" (Matt. 9:13; Mark 2:17; Luke 5:32).

Jesus offered Himself to those who wanted help.

"My mysterious experience a couple of years ago convinced me that God is present and that He cares," Gayle declared. "I was so engulfed in the aurora of God's loving spirit that my whole life changed. The religious life I had was mostly routine ritual to me before that experience, but now I worship because I want to be involved with God. The kind of church is not important. I am there to worship God, not the church. I go where I can find friendly support."

"Me too," says Laura. "I just do not like to go to church where I have to conform to what others say I ought to do. I'll listen to God, but I don't like to be molded into ritualistic righteousness. I listen to my conscience. Is that listening to God?"

Frankl, the psychologist, would say "yes." The trouble with our conscience is that we can so ignore it that it no longer allows God to speak. We can be so proud of our own wisdom that we reject God.

This is worth repeating: "Draw near to God, and He will draw near to you." God will not crash in on us, but "stands at the door and knocks."

Jesse: "Gayle's comment reminded me of a joke I heard a while back: 'Whenever I pass a church, I always pay a visit; because when I get to heaven I do not want St. Peter to say, who is it?' There is just a possibility of truth there."

God cares for you, but He also has given to you the freedom to choose what life you will live. The fact is that we are not capable of handling the full force of His love, so He gives us only as much as we can handle. We never give children more than can be tolerated. It is not that we would deprive the child of anything, but offering too much is frustrating. I think God is like that. He starts where we are, then constantly opens expanding vistas as we grow in our awareness of spiritual things. There is no limit to the possibilities of God.

Turn your question round by asking: "Do I care about God?"

My church used to offer free Christmas meals to
hungry or lonely people. Turkeys with all the trim-
mings were offered. If there remained hungry people
in the community it was because they did not come to
the feast. God has prepared heaven for us, but there
is a requirement: we must come to the feast.

Expect a strange thing to happen when you know
that God cares for you: you'll respect yourself and
begin loving your neighbor. You will begin living in
a peace that passes all understanding.

Not only does God invite you to enter the shelter of His love, He also searches for you to invite
you to come to the feast. Jesus told about sheep in
a fold. Of the hundred sheep, ninety and nine were
safe, but one was lost. The good shepherd would go
out and find the sheep which was lost. Jesus is the
Good Shepherd who cares. He came to seek and to save
that which was lost (Matthew 18:11).

Remember the experience of the disciples on the
Sea of Galilee when a great storm arose and they became afraid? They looked around the boat and found
Jesus asleep. They were frantic! Jesus was rousted
from His sleep as they screamed, "Don't you care if
we perish?" Jesus cared! Not only did He still the
storm, but He quieted their fear (Mark 4:35-41).

Annie Johnson Flint wrote:
> "God hath not promised
> Skies always blue.
> Flower-strewn pathways
> All our lives through.
> God hath not promised
> Sun without rain,
> Joy without sorrow,
> Peace without pain.
>
> But God hath promised
> Strength for the day.
> Rest for the labor,
> Light for the way.
> Grace for the trials,
> Help from above.
> Unfailing sympathy,
> Undying love."

God is always reaching out. **<u>HE CARES!</u>**

WHY DIDN'T GOD JUST MAKE EVERYTHING GOOD?

**"And God saw everything that He had made,
and, behold, it was very good."
Genesis 1:31**

Did you know that verse was in the Bible? What happened?

God created light and darkness. These are still good.

He divided the water above from the water below and created a bubble for the world. This was good.

Then He divided the oceans and the dry lands so that grasses and green things could grow. And these were good.

The sun, moon and stars moved about the heavens so that there were days and seasons. They were good.

When everything was ready, He put all kinds of fish in the oceans and populated the dry lands with animals and birds and creeping things. These, too, were good.

Lastly, He created mankind. Male and female He created, and placed them in paradise, the Garden of Eden. All of that was very good, God said..

That was the end of God's creative actions; but then came the seventh day! God had given Man dominion over the earth. God gave Man a mind with which to freely think. He gave Man choices.

Man changed things!

God did not create stupid puppets. Dolls have no ability to love. God is love. He couldn't create anything but loving people. You can pretend to love someone, but no one can compel you to love.

Since we have been exploring God's nature from many angles, let's study another from the Worldwide Church of God, an organization which claims there is no other true church, but it speaks directly to our question:

"Why hasn't God intervened to end the suffering
of millions of men, women and children?

"Because God has allowed humanity to go its own
way, to develop societies and a way of living apart
from His ways. Humans have reaped the consequences
in untold suffering and death.

"God wants men and women to develop right characters. And character can be developed only through
free moral agency--the freedom to make our personal
decisions--for which we then have to <u>experience the
consequences</u>. In God's plan for humanity, He gives
humans enough time to experience cause and effect.

"God understands that were He to intervene pre-
maturely, people would challenge His intrusion; they
would want to continue in the ways that seem right,
no matter how disastrous the consequences." From THE
PLAIN TRUTH, Dec 1990. (Used by permission.)

Isn't it strange how we demand the right to de-
story ourselves? Of course, we do not intend to
destroy ourselves--we just want what we want!

I entered the Army and had to wear a soldier's
uniform. I felt like a soldier. When I took the uniform off, I no longer felt like a soldier.

God clothed us in paradise. It was very good.

The one thing God could not do with Man was to
demand absolute obedience. That wouldn't be freedom.
That would not have created the potential for love.
However, God does reject us when we choose to do our
"thing" against His will.

"Are you saying that God cannot reverse His own
creative decisions?" asked Jennifer.

It is not the reversal of His decisions that we
are concerned with, is it? Do you want to live your
life in a locked cage? Do you want all of your life
to be controlled as if you were a mindless servant?
How much of our lives are we willing to give up?

Actually, all of God's creative decisions were
good. Even the decision to endow Adam and Eve with
the necessary human ability to make choose for themselves was good. In order to be free to make these
choices, there had to be the possibility to disobey,
to make wrong choices.

The tree of the knowledge of good and evil (the
"apple tree") was necessary. Adam and Eve were not
yet experienced enough to know differences; they had
110

not yet learned to obey God. They could have chosen
not to eat the apple. They could also have remained
naked innocent puppets in the garden, never making a
choice. You would not be here, you see, if they had
been unable to make choices.

David, "That means it is good that they ate the
apple. I can't understand that."

When they ate the apple and learned that they
were naked, were they compelled to hide so God could
not see them? God created them naked. What could be
so wrong about living without clothes? It seems that
what really happened was that they became conscious
of their disobedience; their inner selves were naked
before God.

God did not reject them; they rejected God.

Disobedience engenders fear. Jennifer told us
about her fear that God would punish her if she did
not go to church. Wouldn't you have liked to have a
fig leaf to hide behind so God could not locate you,
Jennifer? All of us sin. All of us pretend we do not
sin, and hope God will accept our pretense. Unless
we get relief from those charades, we find our life
building up with so much guilt that we become unable
to be loving. We try to hide from God.

The greatest of all attempts to hide from God
is to declare there is no God.

When people deny God, they find themselves with
nothing left but to get as much out of this life as
possible. They use their energies for exploiting the
earth, the skies, the animals and other people. All
of living becomes a war zone of selfish pleasure and
greed. Everything becomes mere objects for conquest.
When there isn't any guideline--no heaven to gain or
hell to shun, and only the grave as goal for living
--personal pleasures and the amassing of material
things become life's purpose; the grave its goal.

"Eat, drink and be merry for tomorrow you may
die," said the ancient Greek philosopher, Epicurus.
He did not teach nihilism, the denial of an eternal
existence, but that people should live a joyful life
here on earth.

Then came the "Neo-Epicureans" teaching that it
was only human pleasures which mattered. While I was
in Paris, I met with some of these people. The life
they led was much like that seen among the "hippies"

in San Francisco's "North Beach" artists' colony, or
in Golden Gate Park with the "Peacenics." This type
of living can be found all around the world.

Sartre's movement was called "Existentialism."
He taught that nothing is real to you unless you can
make it exist in your own life. A thing which lived
in you was an "existential" reality. Not that Jean
Paul Sartre advocated living without morals, he said
that each individual had to find what existed, or to
them it did not exist. He did not deny God, neither
did he advocate moral decay. In fact, he said that
the greatest good would be to experience (exist in)
the good of helping other people. His concept was to
bring in a better society.

The ethical God of the Hebrew-Christian religion is not the pattern for gods of other religions.

Romans worshipped Bacchus, the god of wine and
carousing. Bacchanalia orgies are always enticing,
encouraging people to riotous living.

Halloween was initially the religious cleansing
of all evil so celebrating "All-Saints Day" would be
free from contamination. It changed into a Bacchana-
lian festival, a "last fling," a revival of Epicure-
anism.

"Mardi-Gras" began in France as the last chance
to have a party before Lent, a period of fasting before Easter. Fasting was a serious commitment to the
preparation of one's soul as it would experience the
trauma of the crucifixion and the renewal of life in
the resurrection.

"If God had just decreed that everything would
be good, moral, sensible and obedient, we would not
need armies, police, doctors, politicians, lawyers,
psychiatrists, charities, welfare departments along
with other activities involved with easing the ills
and conflicts of humanity," Jesse observed.

On the surface that seems to be ideal, but we
would be mere shadows of reality, as Plato suggested
in his philosophical "Republic." He believed those
gods living on Olympus were the only reality: Earth
was the stage upon which shadows from Olympus could
play. He thought of humanity as being no more actual
than the novels we see portrayed on television sets.
He thought we had no freedom, no individuality--we
are only carbon-copies, clones, of perfection. God
112

could not be pleased with such a world. Shadows can
not respond to His love.

Throughout the Bible, and throughout all other
ethical religions, there are glimpses of God struggling with Man to help build good lives.

Think of these passages:

The "Ten Commandments" are all concerned with
rules for living a good life (Exodus 20:3-15).

"Abhor that which is evil, cleave to that which
is good (Romans 12:9).

"The Lord shall preserve thee from all evil"
(Psalms 121:7).

"Know therefore this day, and consider it in
thine heart, that the Lord, He is God in the heaven
above, and upon the earth beneath: there is none
else. Thou shalt keep therefore His statutes, and
His commandments, which I command thee this day, and
with thy children after thee, and that thou may pro-
long thy days upon the earth, which the Lord thy God
giveth thee forever" (Deuteronomy 4:39,49).

Maybe this will give some understanding to our
question: most of you like modern music and its rock
groups; I don't. Would you be pleased if I were to
command that there be no rock-and-roll performances?
Some of you like hill-billy music, some don't. Some
of you like western songs, some do not. Some of you
like our president, some think he stinks. With all
these differences, how could God make us all happy?
Why doesn't God just allow only "good" music, allow
only the presidents we like?

In many ways, what you think is good is good.

However, God's ways are not flexible. Rebel as
we may, God's eternal love is the basis for His laws
concerning all human actions. Whenever individuals
or mankind move into areas which are not in accord
with the love of God, we get into trouble.

God made everything good. Even our options for
disobeying God are good. By having that option, we
can choose to live in the goodness of God.

"I guess I'm still a bit upset with God," David
thought. "Not only has He made it impossible for us
to prove that He exists, but He created us and gave
us all these urges to satisfy our own natures. And,
that means we constantly put ourselves in danger of
His punishment. No wonder Calvin justified for him-

self why God did what He did. With all that loving
you talk about, it still remains a puzzle to me how
God could have created us to have suffering."

"That's how I used to feel, David," Gayle said
as she put her arm around him. "Now I realize that
when I accept you as my friend, I am also allowing
myself to be at risk of your rejection. You are at
liberty to be what you want to be. I do not compel
you to like me, nor to accept my arm around you."

David shrugged away from her saying: "That will
illustrate my point. It seems to me the world would
be much better off if either we could all like each
other, or could be satisfied to live our lives without worrying if we were doing the right thing. What
is right anyway? What is right for me may not appear
to be the right thing for you."

"That is why we have to be free. That is why we
must live without judgmental demands upon other individuals," Gayle continued to respond. "I believe
God made us bear the responsibility of choices so we
could also know the peace which comes when we understand which way is right.

"Philosophies and psychologies may give answers
to the question, but God always gives the ultimate
answer," Gayle continued. "Jesus repeated the answer
when He was asked about the greatest commandment. To
be brief, I'll just say His answer was to love God,
and to love your neighbor as you love yourself. Not
real easy to comprehend and to put into your own
life."

These discussions were initiated because of the
confusions all of you were expressing. It takes time
to be able to discuss those confusions, doubts and
rejections.

David and Gayle have given us some heavy ideas
to meditate about until next time.

WAS I BORN A SINNER?

"All have sinned and fallen short of the glory of god."Romans 3:23

We are again coming to Paul's discourse on the necessity for coming under the saving grace and love of Jesus Christ. He states, "There is none righteous no, not one" (Rom 3:10). He is stating that there is no such thing as living without doing any wrong.

Perfection is not a human possibility.

Note: there are two distinct usages for "sin."

<u>First</u>, "Sinner" is a title. It is a noun. It has nothing to do with my actions. It has the same meaning as saying that a person is an American or a foreigner; a Jew or a gentile; a Mohammedan or an infidel. I am either "in," or I am "out." Paul uses the name "saints" as the title for Christians, and "sinners" for non-Christians. "Sinner" was also what a social outcast was called. The Hindu equivalent was: "untouchable."

<u>Second</u>, "to sin" is a verb. Used as a verb, it is the action I may take whether I am a Christian or not. All Christians sin, but the fact of our having sinned does not remove us from being "saints."

That is to say, the act of sinning after having accepted Jesus Christ does not cancel salvation.

"Are you saying that if I become baptized I can never be rejected by God?" Jennifer questioned.

There are churches which teach, "once in grace, always in grace." Again, we are into semantics. One attribute of Christianity is living in the joy of a Godly life. What do you think God might say about a person who turned back into a sinful life?

Gayle: "We have been saying all along that God cannot tolerate evil. If God rejects all evil, then a person who once became cleansed through faith, but turned around and became evil again, must have lost the cleansing and must be rejected."

Jesse, "Is that what Paul meant when he wrote that the good the he would do he didn't do, but the things which he shouldn't do, those he found himself doing? I cannot imagine that Paul was saying he felt himself outside of Christianity just because he knew he did some wrong things."

Paul never took glory upon himself. He strongly lifted up the necessity to follow Jesus Christ, and declared that no one should worship him.

"Then, as a title, I guess we were all sinners when we are born," Laura bursts out. "Is that what some churches believe when they baptize babies?"

Maybe we should find what Jesus says about the little children. Do you know what His attitude was about children, Jennifer?

"Sure, Jesus said to let the little children come unto Him for of such is the Kingdom of Heaven," Jennifer replied. "That is in all of the first three Gospels: Matthew, Mark and Luke. And here is another statement related to children: "Unless you become as little children you will in no way enter the Kingdom of Heaven.' I found that in Matthew 18:3."

Who's got a Bible? O.K. Jesse. What does that verse say?

"Almost what Jennifer said. It reads, 'Unless you be converted and become as little children, ye shall in no wise enter into the Kingdom of Heaven.' I'm not sure what being converted meant then."

Good observation, Jesse. Being converted could not have meant conversion to Christianity. John the Baptist could not have baptized for the remission of sins. Jesus must have used the word to indicate the converting of attitudes, a different way of looking at life and each other. Children are trusting, un-biased, loving, unassuming, happy and forgiving. An adult becomes greedy, fearful, doubter, distrustful and defensive. Jesus wasn't talking about conversion from sin, but a conversion to a loving, simple life-style.

Little children do not sin. Sin is related to doing what God says not to do. A child does not yet know the will of God, so is still sinless. There is almost the meaning that a little child is still pure enough to enter the Kingdom of Heaven.

Gayle, "I'd like to ask a question. If a child comes from God, doesn't the child have the spirit of God? If the little child dies, wouldn't his soul be returned to God who gave it? I know that's a problematical question, but it makes me wonder about the new-born babies who die before they have a chance to be baptized."

We are getting a bit away from trying to find God without man-made interpretations, but to answer today's theme we need to discuss this question a bit more.

David is a computer expert. Last week you were asked to see if you could come up with Bible verses to indicate anything about "original sin," or other forms of that phrase. David used the concordance in his computer to search for verses which might refer to sin. He printed out his results for you:

1. "Original sin" is not in the Bible.
2. A sinner from the beginning--not there.
3. Sinner from birth--not in the Bible.
4. Inherited sin--not in the Bible.
5. Inherit sin--not in the Bible.
6. Sins of the father--not in the Bible.
7. Father's sins--not in the Bible.
8. To the third generation--not in the Bible.
9. Down to the fourth generation--not exactly.
10. Sins visited on the children of man--no.
11. This is in the Bible: "Thou shalt not make unto thyself any graven image; Thou shall not bow down thyself unto them, nor serve them: for I the Lord thy God am a jealous God, visiting the iniquity of the fathers upon the children unto the third and fourth generation of them that hate me: and showing mercy unto thousands of them that love me, and keep My commandments" (Genesis 20,4,5,6).
12. "By one man sin entered into the world" (Rom. 5:12).
13. Conceived in sin--not in the Bible.
14. "He that committeth sin is of the devil, for the devil sinneth from the beginning" (1 John 3:8).
15. "All have sinned and fallen short of the glory of God" (Romans 3:23).

"I couldn't find any place which declared that we are sinners at birth, except the interpretation Laura proposed," David added.

Paul discusses God's foreknowledge and predestination in Romans 8:29,30. He also discussed that God ordained before the world that certain actions would happen (I Corinthians 2:7). I am afraid that it would do us little good to discuss these passages because they have been pivotal points between those who believe that everything was predestinated (fore-ordained) by God, and those who believe that God put within us a free will with which to respond to Him, and with which to make choices for our own lives in the sense of Joshua when he admonished:

"If it seem evil unto you to serve the Lord, choose ye this day whom ye will serve; whether the gods which your fathers served on the other side of the flood, or the gods of the Amorites, in whose land ye dwell: but as for me and my house, we will serve the Lord" (Joshua 24:15,16).

What did the rest of you find?

Jesse: "John 3:15-21 discusses the purpose of Jesus. He came to save those who were lost, but it seems to speak of condemnation as something we have done--something we are responsible for."

Jennifer: "John 6:64 says that Jesus knew from the beginning who would not believe, and who would betray Him. As I read the rest of that chapter, it seemed to me that Jesus knew about these things from the beginning of His ministry, not from the time of creation."

David: "I found in Acts 15:18 that God is aware of all His works from the beginning of the world. It seems to say that God _knows_ all about us, but it did not impress me as saying God had predestined all the possible happenings of the universe."

Laura: "Galatians 2:16 through 3:26 talks about whether we are justified by our good works and obedience to the law, or by faith in Jesus Christ. Paul even called the Galatians foolish because they were struggling to be perfect by keeping the ancient Law. They were constantly condemning themselves for being imperfect. Paul declared that they had suffered in vain."

Gayle: "The passage in Romans 5:1-21 says that Christ died for us while we were yet sinners and had no strength to save ourselves. That says to me that I have to make the choice of accepting God's grace. Paul didn't mince words when he declared that by one man's disobedience many (all) were made sinners, so by the obedience of one many will be made righteous.
118

That reminded me of Acts 4:12 which says: 'There is no other name given among men, whereby we must be saved.'"

What do these verses tell us about being born in sin? We could keep ourselves busy searching for many other verses, of course. For example, the Old Testament constantly telling the people that IF they would return to God, they would be forgiven and have all sorts of blessings.

Being right with God is not just a concern for Christians; being on good terms with the Law of God is basic to the Old Testament.

Being on good terms with whatever god might be honored in a particular religion is of paramount importance to those people. Even satanic cults emphasize being on good terms with their god, the devil!

Our question becomes: if we are born in sin, is fate our only destiny? Or are we born innocent children having to choose to come into God's grace?

Personally, I believe in a God who would create only loving persons. God is not the source of evil.

It is not His will that any should perish. We went through that in a previous discussion.

One of the first explanations I was given concerning sin was that a new-born child was like a new sheet of typing paper--no smears or mistakes--just a clean sheet of paper. The power of sin entered human existence when "Adam" chose to go against God's law. I didn't inherit Adam's guilt, but all of humanity was evicted from the Garden of Eden--out of Paradise --it became the option for each person to choose the redemption of Christ, or to stay out of paradise.

When must we choose? Jesus said that whosoever would could come. That involves being old enough to make the choice, and old enough to know what choice to make.

The Roman Catholic Church gives confirmation at the age of twelve. Jesus was twelve when he entered the temple of Jerusalem and started teaching. In the Hebrew religion the age of twelve was established as the time a child becomes a responsible adult, a time when he becomes a "man" and could be counted as one of the members in the worship services. Jesus didn't state any age, but offered salvation to all who believed on Him.

For those who believe an individual must make an "adult" choice to accept Christ and be baptized, the age varies from about six years to twelve years as the age for accepting Christ. My problem with a young age is that I cannot imagine a child only six years old becoming convinced of sin and responsibly asking for forgiveness and salvation.

I do not believe a child is condemned before it can make a choice. The child must first learn what it means to sin before it can make a choice. I respect those who point out that we can commit sin before knowing anything about God. Ignorance about God is not bliss. The consequences of sin are probably comprehended when the child is about ten years old.

There is also the other side of being a sinner; it is the title which identifies a non-Christian.

Then there is the universal question regarding those who live out their lives without ever having heard about Christian salvation.

I am thankful that I am not eternity's judge!

All I can believe is that no one is born into the Kingdom of God. Our genes do not carry a trait of salvation.

Likewise, I do not believe our genes carry the guilt of sinning through which we are caused us to inherit eternal condemnation.

You will be confronted with such questions for the rest of your lives. Know what you believe, and have a basis for your belief. Do not be twisted by every wind of doctrine which blows across you. Have your own assurance in the consistency and salvation of God.

DOES THE DEVIL CAUSE ME TO DO EVIL?

"And Eve said, The serpent did beguile me, and I did eat."

Genesis 3:13

When Martin Luther, the German Catholic priest who is credited with starting the reformation which is now called Protestantism, was excommunicated, he was hidden by a friend in a dungeon cell to save his life. There he did a lot of heavy meditating.

He was so overwhelmed at mankind's sinning that he sought answers from God, but he got only stronger convictions that all religious practices ought to be purified and restored to the teachings of Jesus.

Historic accounts tell that one day while deep in his meditations Satan appeared before him to try to convert him. Martin Luther rejected the Devil so violently that he threw his inkwell at him. If you were to visit the dungeon, you would discover a blot on the wall which, you will be told, is the ink that passed through the Devil and splashed onto the wall.

"That may be a good story," David reacted, "but I have been taught in school that there isn't such a thing as a devil."

"Not only that," Jesse added, "but where could a devil come from? Wouldn't God have to create such a being? You see, I missed the class two weeks ago, but this doesn't make sense, especially with all the talking we have been doing about God not being able to create evil."

"Yes, and if God cannot make us act evil, then where do I get the drive to do things my way rather than do what God wants me to do?" Jennifer asked.

Laura: "A few weeks ago I went to a church and heard the preacher telling that the end of the world was coming soon. He preached that just before the "second coming" there would be this period of seven years during which the anti-Christ would dictate to the world. He said the devil would make everybody live in sin but they would think they were doing

God's will. Anyone, he said, who tried to maintain a Christian life according to the Bible, would be persecuted and martyred. That sounds like he believes in a devil who is trying to get us to disobey God."

"When we pray The Lord's Prayer in church, we ask that God will not lead into temptation. Can God ever make us go into temptations?" Jesse asked.

We need to stop and deal with Jesse's question. I have read many interpretations about that part of the prayer. One writer suggests that leading us into temptation is God's way of testing us: God gives the temptations to test us and see if we are strong enough to withstand them. The writer did not imply that God would be forcing us to do evil.

Another writer suggests that the phrase should read, "Let us not be led into temptation." Here we seem to pray to God to keep us from being led by any other power. With God's protection the devil could not manipulate us into yielding to temptations.

A third writer tries to be funny (maybe) when he points out that were God to lead us into temptation, He would have to be ahead of us and already in that temptation.

Jesus had just given the prayer which included: "Forgive us our debts (transgressions) as we forgive our debtors (those who transgress against us)."

Transgressions are a type of sin. They are the social evils. Transgressions are not acts of love: they are selfishness--breaking the tenth Commandment that we must not covet what belongs to our neighbor. It seems to me that Jesus was directing our thoughts to understand that when we transgress against those neighbors, we transgress against God.

Jesse asked a very normal question about where the devil came from. Every theologian and student of the Bible eventually comes to this question, but there is no real answer. Theologians of all faiths everywhere have tried to solve the riddle with the same remaining mystery.

The closest answer comes from the book of Job, the first chapter, which tells about a conference in heaven at which satan appeared. God inquires as to where Satan came from. Satan says that he has come from walking to and fro upon the earth. This gives rise to the speculation that God created "beings" on
122

the earth prior to mankind. Satan had been honored
in heaven. There is nothing in this passage to lead
us to conclude that satan (Lucifer) was created
evil.

God allowed Satan to test Job to see if he had
the strength to remain faithful. It is a story worth
reading.

Don't get me wrong. At the time of the meeting
in heaven, Satan had been cast out of heaven because
he had rebelled and tried to become the head God. It
may be that God was testing to see if Satan might be
reformed. After all, here was Lucifer again appearing in heaven where only holy persons could be.

The book of Job is notably amazing because here
is a complex cosmic picture at a time when mankind
thought the world was flat--and not very large.

Later, Isaiah wails: "How thou art fallen from
heaven, O Lucifer, son of the morning" (Isaiah 14:
12). Lucifer says: "I will exalt my throne above the
stars of God, I will be like the Most High."

The origin of evil was self-adulation by Satan.
His egotistical declaration of becoming equal to God
and having power to be in competition to God, caused
him to be thrown out of heaven. The angels of heaven
had been created spirits of love, with a freedom to
respond to God's love. Satan chose to strive with
God and try to become even superior to God.

The reality of the devil is strongly depicted
in both the Old Testament and the New Testament.

Baal, or Baalim, was the pagan god of idols. He
represented ungodliness. Baal was similar to the god
of Roman merriment, Bacchus. He is the playful Pan
of the Greek Neo-Epicureans.

Paul wrote against an "eat, drink and be merry"
philosophy of the Cretians, warning Christians not
to be like them. The practices of Baal worship which
included idolatry, meat offerings, human sacrifices
of both young women and babies, offerings of riches
and wild rites of drunkenness and pagan pleasures.

There was constant conflict between the priests
of Baal and the prophets of Jehovah. The Israelites
were in the center of the conflict.

It is much easier to cause people to fear something than it is to build up a loving nature. Don't
we fear the dark and whatever mystical demons might

be lurking there? We become afraid when black cats
cross our path. I still remember: "step on a crack
and you'll break your mother's back."

The pioneers crossing the Great Plains needed
salt for survival, or for trading with the indians.
It couldn't be obtained in the wilderness. To spill
any salt was to bring on bad luck, but tossing a bit
of salt over your right shoulder removed it. Luck,
fate, God, and Satan were constant companions of our
pioneer ancestors.

Among the 330 million gods of India there must
be over half of them representing fears, sicknesses,
death and destructive fate. Siva (Shiva), depicted
as having many arms, is one of the higher goddesses
in the Hindu religion. She is the goddess of war, as
well as the goddess of reproduction and fertility.

I cherish the story of the missionary who went
into the primitive tribes of Africa and preached of
"hell-fire and brimstone." It scared those natives
into becoming Christians. They did not want such a
terrible fate. The missionary returned home for his
sabbatical, then went back to his missionary field.
He found the natives having elaborate ceremonies for
Satan, the devil.

"Why are you doing this?" he cried.

"Oh," they replied. "You told us all about the
Jesus who loved us and was kind and forgiving; we're
not afraid of Him. It is that terrible old devil we
had to try to please so he wouldn't cause those evil
things you told us about."

Jesus started His ministry with the three temptations of the devil: power, protection, and riches.

The devil entered into the heart of Judas, making him betray Jesus (John 13:2). Scholars do not
agree upon the personality of Judas; some contend he
was a misbeguided zealot who attempted to force the
coming of the Kingdom of God. Others propose that he
was an honest follower until Satan entered into him,
causing him to betray Jesus for the thirty pieces of
silver, maybe worth about three thousand of today's
dollars--some scholars will evaluate that silver at
about three hundred dollars.

The Book of Ephesians gives a warning: "Neither
give place to the devil" (4:27). Can you imagine how
the people interpreted Paul's warning?
124

In the case of Ananias and Saphira, Peter says, "Satan filled your heart to lie to the Holy Ghost" (Acts 5:43).

Notice that none of the Gospel writers, including Paul, Peter, James and John allowed any room for doubt that Satan was very active in the world.

All types of sick people were brought to Jesus. Jesus chased the devil from them; they became well.

The name "devil" is named 46 times in the New Testament. "Satan" is mentioned 18 times in the Old Testament and 37 times in the New Testament.

We are told to be forever alert to temptations of the devil, and that he can transform himself into an angel of light, even into a resemblance of Jesus so that people will be misled (2 Cor. 11:4).

Critics against Christianity are not new. Some scholars believe that the Gospel of John was written to prove the reality of Jesus, and to emphasize the activity of the devil.

Atheists have always denied any form of super-beings; they deny the devil as well as denying God. Many sociologists and psychiatric practitioners are humanists, so must deny an actual devil. There are numerous "modern" and humanistic ministers who also deny the existence of a devil.

Logic and the consistency of God tells us that if the voice of God speaks within us, then the voice of evil must also speak within us. To believe Jesus is basic for Christian faith. Jesus warned against the wiles (cunningness) of the devil. Doubt is one of the cunning ways the devil uses for getting us to lose faith in God.

James advised: "Resist the devil and he will flee from you" (James 4:7).

The answer to this discussion's question would be: "Yes, the devil tempts you, but you have God's power to overcome the temptations."

Paul encourages the Christians to remain faithful: "There hath no temptation taken you but such is common to man; but God is faithful, who will not suffer you to be tempted above that ye are able; but will with the temptation also make a way to escape, that ye may be able to bear it" (I Cor. 10:13).

The devil's temptations will always be enticing to you. You will even sin at times because of them.

But remember, Your relationship with God is through
the free gift of salvation provided by Jesus Christ.
Your sins can be forgiven, and no one can take your
membership in God's Kingdom of Heaven away from you.

It is possible for you to become like the "Man
Without A Country" and live forever in a space where
there is no home. But, like that man in the novel,
you must reject that homeland yourself.

This phrase from the Philippines bears repeating: "It's up to you."

The devil has the power and cunningness to put
enticing temptations before you, but he cannot make
you yield to those temptations.

The comment about Satan entering into Judas was
a conditional temptation. Judas had to accept that
invasion or it would not have been effective.

Here is a closing thought: if the devil can not
force himself on you, a similar self-restriction is
upon God. God is able to manipulate, but does not.
The devil has none of these powers!

Jesse: "One more thing disturbs me about Satan.
I know we discussed that he would be bound for that
thousand years, but what happens after that?"

You almost had me there, Jesse. Going back to
the origin of Satan, we realize that Satan was also
created. Since Satan had a beginning and moves with
time the same as we do, it is obvious that he is not
eternal. Therefore, when time is no more and all is
returned to the eternity of God's pure love, nothing
will remain of evil.

You and I will have an eternity without sin or
temptations. It seems to me that just as we will be
purged and made to be as the angels, Satan will be
purged of evil also as he rejoins God in eternity.

Purging Satan would be similar to the ending of
the wicked city of Nineveh: evil was eliminated, but
the city lived on.

God is eternally everywhere and pervades everything. Satan would have to be infused with the sinlessness of God. Eternity would not contend between
good and evil: there would be no evil. There would
be no more free-will because pure love is absolute.

I rejoice that Gayle is able to tape these sessions so I will be able to listen to what I've just
said!

126

WHO WAS JESUS?

"Thou art the christ, the Son of the Living God."
Matthew 16:16

This will not be an easy discussion. The person of Jesus has been discussed, argued over, rejected and fantasized about ever since He appeared in the manger of Bethlehem.

Oh, hello there, Amanda. Back with your grandmother for Easter this time?

"Yes. I especially wanted to come and hear what would be discussed today. Laura phoned me and told me about this discussion topic. Will I disturb the group if I ask some questions which you may have already have covered?"

You certainly won't bother me. How about the rest of you? You see, you are free to ask questions whenever you choose.

First, let me set a little background about the debates concerning the person of Jesus. It does not do any good to close our eyes and ears and pretend that everyone agrees with Peter's "Good Confession." It may be hard to believe, but there are many interpretations about what Peter meant.

My professor of homiletics (preaching) refused to let us use the Gospel of John because he thought it to be a fantasy concocted to counteract Gnostics who advocated that Jesus was only a human who taught basic religious philosophies. My professor was not an agnostic, but the first verse of John had him so confused that he rejected it. He could not envision that Jesus was the Word which created the world.

Scholars who have studied Hinduism propose that Jesus may have been educated in India during His unknown years (nothing in the Bible tells of His life from age 12 to His starting His ministry at age 30), because His teachings were so similar to what Hinduism had been teaching for several hundred years.

Caesar thought that Jesus had come to establish a political empire which might overthrow the powers of Rome. Caesar not only caused every male child to

be slaughtered to eliminate any potential political
threat, but later, the power of Rome gave consent to
the death of Jesus. Caesar saw Jesus to be real and
an important person.

The established Jewish religion rejected Jesus
because He did not teach their rituals. They would
not accept Jesus as the promised messiah, but held
that He was a divisive, upsetting charlatan.

Modern critics of religions point out that many
religious leaders of the past have been deified and
given virgin births. These growing glorifications of
past leaders took hundreds of years to evolve and be
attached to such persons. In Jesus' case, writings
of His life was just a few years after His death by
persons living during His lifetime.

What we've been trying to do, Amanda, is to see
what insights we may gain as we study God's reality,
then build our faith around our experiences. We may
learn from the experiences of other people, but until we personalize the experiences they have little
power in our lives. We read the Bible, but atheists
also read the Bible without comprehending its truth,
rejecting it as if it were only imaginative fables
concocted to express the wishes or fears of mankind.
Preconceived ideas blind us to the truth.

We also have to recognize the immensity of God
and the infinite individual diversities among people
to know that our own pathway is only one of a myriad
of pathways to God.

Amanda: "But aren't there basic truths directing which way our paths should go? there must also
be some false directions. Maybe you have discussed
these directions before, but I just had to ask."

And this discussion period offers you a grand
opportunity to review some of those basics. We have
said the Ten Commandments have basic religious and
social truths, but legalistically keeping the commandments can leave us short of having the spirit of
loving God and loving our neighbors as we love ourselves.

"Isn't loving ourselves what we've been talking
about as being selfish and destructive?" Jesse wondered. "We seem to settle something in one talking,
then our next discussion changes what we just said.
I am trying to keep up with the changes, but it is
128

confusing. You keep saying that God is consistent, but are we being consistent?"

Loving yourself does not mean the same as being in love with yourself. Jesus meant that we must be so at ease with ourselves that we can reach out and love our neighbors. Accepting ourselves for what we are, not for what we think we want to be, is one of the secrets of happiness.

The Ten Commandments are like a candle glowing in the darkness by which we can find our way and do our work. Jesus said He did not come to destroy the commandments, but to fulfill them. We need light to overcome darkness. When the sun shines, it does not cancel the need which the candle tried to meet, but gives such an abundance of light that a ritualistic carrying of a lighted candle around with you has no more usefulness.

"Why was Jesus able to give such light? I know that He said He was the light of the world, and that we are to be lights for the world, but what made Him claim such a position? Was He seeking to be honored among men?" David wondered.

You have asked nearly the same question which was asked by the disciples, "Who are you, Jesus?" He answered by first asking what other people were saying about Him. They answered that some thought Him to be Elijah, Moses, Solomon, or some other prophet. He had been intimate with them a long time, so they were witnesses when He fed the multitudes. They saw Him walking on water, stilling the storm, resurrecting the dead, making the lame to walk, and causing the blind to see. They had listened to His amazing revelations about God.

The time had come to reveal who He really was.

It is easy for us to say that someone else did something, but there comes a time for us to settle in our own hearts what we believe. It is necessary that we become comfortable expressing our beliefs.

How would you have answered Jesus as He asked, "Who do you say that I am?"

Peter, the impetuous, enthusiastically replied: "Thou art the Christ, the Son of the living God."

Let's put on the chalkboard some of the things you would call Jesus. Just give me the words and I will write them down.

Saviour	Messiah	Redeemer
Friend	My example	Son of God
Healer	Spirit	Miracle-
Compassionate	Immanuel	worker
Strong	Sensitive	Human being
Teacher	Prophet	Forgiving
Patient	Independent	Sociable
Forgiving	Strong	Practical
Confident	Burden bearer	Holy
Mystical	Loving	Courageous

That should be enough for the moment. What do all these words mean? I see that you have put both human and spiritual characteristics there. That is good. I think we should look upon Jesus as having a dual nature--being both human and divine.

On the one hand, He was the obedient child born in Bethlehem who grew in wisdom and stature and in favor with God and man. On the other hand, He said: "I and my Father are one." When He healed the sick man who had been lowered through the roof by friends and said, "Thy sins are forgiven," those around Him challenged His authority declaring that only God had the authority to forgive sins. Jesus asked them if it was easier, to say, "thy sins be forgiven," or to say, "be ye healed."

They mumbled among themselves saying that fools could pretend to forgive sins--there could be no way of proving it! To tell the man he was healed was an entirely different matter, because the proof must be right there. The event terminates as Jesus says: "I say to thee: arise, and take up thy bed, and go thy way into thine house" (Mark 2:1-12).

Immediately the sick man arose, took up the bed and walked out among the doubters. Can you picture the rejoicing the healed man had with his friends!

I can't help but wonder how many of the people present there caught what Jesus had just revealed to them. The scoffers had declared that only God could forgive sins. Jesus told the man that his sins were forgiven, then He proved His authority over sin with the miracle of instant healing. Jesus demonstrated that He was God.

You look amazed, Amanda. I know the group has been preparing for this discussion, but you appeared shocked by such a direct statement.

130

"Not so much shocked," Amanda responded. "I was awed. I have read a few passages about Jesus being the Son of God, but I never really visualized what I read. I even read John 10:30 where Jesus says that He and His Father are one. I'd like for you to tell us what you believe about Jesus."

Fair enough. But first, let me first tell you who I am, or what makes me think the way I do. I am a practical, down-to-earth logical thinker. I have the curiosity of a scientist. Adventuring is such a natural part of me that I would like to "go where no man has gone before" (T.V. series STAR TREK). I like people, but there are times when I seek the solitude of the mountains, or ocean shores.

Then there is the other side of me. I believe in miracles and mystical experiences. I believe in God so encompassing us so that we hear His voice, a voice usually heard as our conscience or intuition. Sometimes we may have dreams which give us a vivid communication. Psychologists experiment with E.S.P. with which people receive communications from other people by mental telepathy or receptiveness. Is it possible that E.S.P. is actually the universal communication of God's spirit?

That may seem to make me quite strange, having one part of me being very practical and logical, and the other part reaching to the mystery of theology.

You asked me what I think of Jesus. I believe He was God taking on a form of humanity in order to share experiences and teach God's ways at a definite location at a finite moment of time. Put it another way: the physical Jesus lived here on earth while He continued to pervade the cosmos as the eternal God.

I believe that the everlasting God so loved the world that He came into the world as Jesus so whosoever believeth on Him (i.e., accept Him) should not perish but have everlasting life (John 3:16).

Jesus, to me, was both human and divine.

Jesus was in time, but He exists eternally.

Jesus suffered as a human and became a perfect sacrifice to take away the sins of the world.

Jesus had the wisdom of the omniscient God, but his human mind increased in wisdom and human understanding. The statement that He grew in favor with God and man reveals His dual nature.

The humanity of Jesus appeared to constantly be renewed by His communions with "My Father." He knew we needed that communication, so He taught us how to pray.

Jesus was unique. He never sinned so needed no forgiveness. Being sinless, He could become a spotless sacrifice for our sins. The Old Testament law required sacrifices to be pure and spotless.

Here are some passages for you to look up and see what they say about the uniqueness of Jesus:

"I am the way, the truth, and the life. No man cometh unto the Father but by me" (John 14:6).

"I am the door, if any man enter in he shall be saved" (John 10:9).

"He that believeth and is baptized shall be saved, but he that believeth not shall be damned" (Mark 16:16).

"Neither is there salvation in any other: for there is none other name under heaven given among men, whereby we must be saved" (Acts 4:12).

Could Jesus have escaped the cross? No way!

Jesus came into humanity and time for a definite purpose. His divine love could never escape the consequences of His purpose in coming to earth. His human body cringed at the thought of the cross, but His spirit could not turn away.

Jesus Christ. Son of God. Blessed Redeemer!

Hear the everlasting invitation: "The Spirit and the bride say Come. And let him that is athirst come. And whosoever will, let him take of the water of life freely" (Rev. 22:17).

"GOD (JESUS) IS NOT WILLING THAT ANY SHOULD PERISH" (2 Peter 3:9).

"Before we leave, I'd like to know what you thought of OMNI's August, 1991, issue with the cover heading: THE SEARCH FOR GOD?" Gayle asked.

That was a very enlightening issue dealing with the vastness and unimaginable distances of space. I was intrigued with the new discoveries, but the big mistake of science is to search for God by physical means. God cannot be found by using a test-tube.

Keep in mind what the Pope said about searching for facts, recognizing that only faith can find God.

WHAT DOES IT MEAN TO BE SAVED?

"He that believeth and is baptized shall be saved."
Matthew 16:16

Let's start with an illustration: suppose that we are all nature lovers out in the wilderness when a devastating storm suddenly comes upon us. There is no place to escape. The blizzard brings only certain death. A stranger appears and tells us that he has prepared a way of escape; he has built a storm-proof shelter, but we must follow him.

We are knowledgeable people. We know how to get through jungles and forests; we know how to go over mountains and across burning deserts; we know how to protect ourselves during snow storms and devastating heat. Are we to admit to this stranger that we are lost and in fear of our lives? Can we become willing to follow a way which is different from the way we have so carefully plotted for ourselves?

The stranger knows our dilemma and says, "Whosoever will may come."

When Jesus told parables, some disciples would request explanations. I don't feel bad, therefore, in asking for someone to explain my story.

Jesse: "It seems that you have included several items. The story implies that our lost condition is not be our fault, but is a natural occurrence."

Laura: "I see the stranger as having compassion for people. Coming out in the storm exposed him also to the dangers of the blizzard. If a blizzard raged outside my nice cozy shelter, I imagine I'd probably choose to remain inside. And, how could the stranger know the group was out there anyway?"

"I was caught in a blizzard once," Amanda said. "I would not have believed that a blinding storm can disorientate you. Even our leader could not decide which direction we were going. We did not know how to get home. Those of us who have had some hiking experience and training were convinced that we knew where we were going--but we did not agree with each other. I felt the dilemma of the group. They were probably only half conscious and began to huddle so

they could have mutual comfort. The entire group
could have died of the cold."

Your experience, Amanda, adds depth to the illustration. All illustrations have a point. What is
this story illustrating?

Gayle: "It seems to me that it was an allegory
to show the purpose of Jesus. Jesus had not caused
them to get lost. He did not remove the storm. They
were not picked up and moved to safety. He did not
argue with them. He didn't even prove that He had a
shelter. His presence showed that He cared. He had
to know how to find them as well as how to lead them
to safety. It is interesting that the stranger gave
each of them the choice to follow him."

That's about it, Gayle. Foreigners can live in
your land but they aren't citizens until they accept
the new land and are sworn in. Many people who come
to churches and enjoy the fellowship and activities
there never accept membership into Christ. They are
still "lost."

There are children in all the developing countries who never have enough to eat; never get diets
which are proper nourishment; live with the fear of
conflict; grow up with physical, emotional and mental handicaps; they become exploited by governments
and other helpers. They are truly lost.

Suppose there comes into their midst a stranger
bringing food to save them from hunger; doctors come
to save them from their sicknesses; teachers come to
save them from ignorance. Others come with offers to
save them by moving them to a country where there is
no poverty, hunger, disease or fears. Would you expect them to want to be "saved"?

One of the purposes of Jesus was to show how to
live abundant and happy lives. He gave the command
to love one another. He said to visit those who are
sick, befriend those in prisons, feed the hungry, be
a friend, clothe the naked and give shelter to those
who were homeless or orphans. To be saved indicates
there was a lost condition, but now you are safe.

Jesus taught obedience to the government, obedience to God, payments for hired workers, a settling
of debts, being humble, living a religious life, be
witnesses so others could know how to live in God's
love.

134

Jesus' conflict with the priests and religious leaders was not because He taught wrong beliefs, but because He taught such intense individual devotions to God, in place of just obedience to the rituals of the temple. God's laws were good, but the interpretation of those laws had made them lose their power.

The question asked about, "Who is my neighbor?" involved one of those interpretations. Jesus taught about love for one's neighbor. The law about caring for your neighbor and not to covet what belonged to your neighbor had been interpreted to mean no one is my neighbor unless his land touches mine.

How many neighbors could have land that touched mine? The person whose land did not actually touch mine could be cheated, robbed, sold bad goods, etc. Stingy misers didn't want to treat even their close neighbor honestly, so they made an additional interpretation: roads separate property; therefore, if I build a road all around my property, I will have no neighbor to worry about since no land touches mine!

You can understand the anger against Jesus when He told the story of the good Samaritan and declared than everybody was your neighbor. His illustration said there was no escape from living as a neighbor.

We discussed the implications of Paul's statement that all have sinned and fallen short of God's glory. It is impossible for me, or for you, to live a perfect life. Since the wages of sin is death, am I to be eternally condemned?

You know John 3:16, so I'll just mention that Jesus came for the purpose of saving the "lost."

Jesus came because mankind was lost in a deadly blizzard of life. Mankind wasn't able to save itself from death. God had spoken to prophets and saints of various cultures from the beginning of humanity, but mankind was not capable of understanding the things God revealed.

Finally, God appeared in Jesus. He lived and taught. He suffered. He became the sacrifice for our salvation when He gave Himself on the cross.

"I need a listing of what it means to be saved. I understand what we have been discussions, but it would be helpful to have it put together. I would like some compact statements. Could we condense the New Testament?" Jennifer asked almost jokingly.

Can the New Testament be condensed? Certainly, but such an effort could lead to a dogma, and dogmas have ways of crystallizing and ruining the spirit.

Let's have a "bull-session" with a free flow of responses from all of you. Speak out about what it means to be a Christian.

"To be saved means to be freed from fear."

"It means to have loving companions, and to be a loving companion."

"I like to think of it as being willing to be a servant. All my life I have heard about bearing my cross, but it was something I did not understand. I hated to be told that. I think the meaning of being saved is the joyous acceptance of whatever comes into my life."

"Having an eternal life fulfilling the promise of being saved. I am glad we discussed the different ideas people have about heaven. Now I am comfortable with knowing that eternal life is such an amazingly great thing that I don't have to explain it to anyone, not even to myself."

"I like the feeling from actually knowing Jesus saved me."

"The meaning of being saved? I have been lost. Believe me, there is nothing compared to the thrill of knowing everything is right with you."

"How about the song which says I am safe in the arms of Jesus?"

"The meaning of being saved means to me that my present life now has purpose and meaning. Christ is like a secure rudder on a ship in a storm."

Each of us will have our own definitions. You gave some good responses.

Jesse had another problem, "After I have accepted Jesus, will I be lost if I sin again?"

That will be the subject of our coming session. All of you may want to make some research this week on Jesse's question.

CAN I LOSE MY SALVATION?

"There is a sin unto death"
1 John 5:16

At the last session you were invited to search the Bible to see if you could find any references to losing your salvation. What did you find?

"I suppose you expected me to use my computer," David responded. "It probably isn't right for me to take up the whole evening with the number of references I found, but let me start with a reference from the Old Testament. It is in Deuteronomy 6:3-15, one of the passages recording the Ten Commandments. God had directed Moses to lead the Israelites from Egypt where the miracles of plagues took place; He made it possible to escape the Egyptian army by parting the Red Sea; and directed them to the Promised Land. It would be logical for them to have been faithful and devoted to God, but the 12th verse contains a warning: 'beware lest thou forget the Lord which brought you up out of the land of Egypt.' Could this verse indicate that after they were saved, they could become lost?"

Jennifer: "How about the story about the house that had a devil cast out of it, but no good spirits were put into the emptiness. When that evil spirit came back and found it empty, he called seven of his fellow evil spirits to come and live there, causing the house to became worse than it was at first. You will find the story in Matthew 12:43-45. Isn't Jesus warning that just being cleansed is not enough?"

Both of you have made good observations, but we should hear from everybody before making comments.

Gayle: "How can David's question be compare to Jesus' statement in John 6:37; 'All that the Father giveth me, I will in no wise cast out'? I attended a certain church a few years ago, and heard a sermon that said once you were in grace you would always be in grace. It said that no matter what you did after you were saved, you would not lose your salvation."

Jesse: "When Lot's wife was saved out of Sodom
with the rest of Lot's family, they had been warned
by God not to look back. She may have wanted to see
the fireworks, or she may have been yearning to have
the social life she had back in the city, but as she
looked back, disobeying God, she was changed into a
pillar of salt. She was saved by obedience to God,
but she was lost when she disobeyed. It is interesting to listen to people who have visited the Israel
 tell about going to the Dead Sea being shown a tall
rock which is claimed to have been Lot's wife. That
is not once in grace, always in grace."

Laura: "I read John 6:37. I agree with Gayle's
thought. We have eternal salvation when we're saved
by Jesus Christ. However, some of my friends tell me
that I can lose my salvation. How can there be any
sense out of two such different ideas?"

David again: "Luke 17:12 tells of Jesus healing
ten lepers who had to go wash their eyes in the pool
of Siloam. Only one returned to praise God. Did this
mean that nine of the men who had been restored to
health did not have their hearts open to God so that
they were not saved even though they were cleansed?"

Jennifer: "How about Jesus' statement about the
man who started to plow, but turned back, so is not
fit to enter into the Kingdom of Heaven? That reference is Luke 9:62, but it's also found in the other
Gospels. Is this what some people call backsliding?
Is backsliding the same as losing my salvation?"

Gayle: "I'd like to add the scolding Paul gave
the Galatians. In the second chapter he writes that
when we accept Christ we are dead to the law of sin
and death. Some teachers had followed Paul, declaring that you had to keep Jewish laws in order to be
a Christian. Paul writes in the third chapter: 'O
foolish Galatians, who has bewitched you that you
should not obey the truth?' In the third verse he
continued: 'Are ye so foolish? Having begun in the
Spirit, are ye now made perfect by the flesh?"

"Oh, I'm sorry about carrying on like this, but
when I read the book of Galatians I seems like I am
reading my own life. Even though the Galatians had
been saved, they had turned to perfecting themselves
through Jewish laws. Did they thereby lose the sal-
tion they had received through Jesus Christ?"
138

As David said, there are many verses which bear on this subject; let us stop and consider some them, as well as the questions you have presented here.

In the first place, the references from the Old Testament do not relate to Christian salvation.

The Old Testament relates to obedience to God as stated in the Ten Commandments and other revelations given to the prophets. God's blessings were for persons as well as for the nation.

Disobedience brought punishment. Returning to God by obedience brought blessings, but being acceptable to God was not a life-long condition. It contained no eternal salvation.

David's question about the ten lepers is vital and pertinent to our topic. It would be as if some church were to offer shelter to homeless persons. It would open its doors to whosoever would come. Each person would have the responsibility of choosing to accept or to reject that salvation. Just because the church was open and they were in the church did not mean that they would be saved. There are many people who join the church for its benefits, but they never honor God. They are not saved if they merely belong to some church. The nine lepers who did not return to praise God were healed, but it is clear that they did not receive salvation.

Let's take up Gayle's question about the Galatians. Did Paul indicate that the Galatians had to be condemned for their foolishness? Here is a vital point: they were foolish, but not lost. Even we may become foolish at times!

Ministers can become entangled as easily as any one else in the lure of prestige obtained by knowledge and titles. I know. I had to work to get my college degree. I used the G.I. Bill so I could go to seminary and get a Master degree. Extra work in the Chaplaincy gave me my Doctorate. I can now feel something of what Paul must have felt. Although he was taught by the most learned man of his times, he says that he counts all things but loss in order to put on Jesus Christ. Counselors are constantly advising people to get their priorities straight.

I certainly do not mean that you should not get the greatest education you can attain. God utilizes all the talent you can develop as He builds through

you, but you need to remember that the great secret
of happiness is in forgetting yourself and living in
the love of God. Persons without any schooling can
live in love; they can receive salvation.

Jesus called "ignorant" fishermen to be disciples. He also called a wealthy tax collector and a
physician to be His disciples.

Jesus states in John 6:37: "All that the Father
gives unto me, I will in no wise cast out." It can
be looked at with two perspectives. First, He is not
talking about predestination. Second, He does not
propose that no matter what I do or think I will not
be rejected.

This leads us to look to Paul's statement that
there is a sin unto death (Rom. 6:16 or 1 John 5:16)
and link it with Jesus' statement in Matt. 12:31,32:
"All manner of sin and blasphemy shall be forgiven
unto men; but the blasphemy against the Holy Ghost
shall not be forgiven unto men. And whosoever speaketh a word against the Son of man, it shall be forgiven him; but whosoever speaketh against the Holy
Ghost, it shall not be forgiven him, neither in this
world, neither in the world to come."

Maybe it would be proper to warn you like Paul
would have done: don't be foolish and turn away from
Jesus Christ because you trust in your own wisdom.

You can become lost!

You are responsible for your own salvation. It
isn't your good works, but your good faith which has
power to sustain your salvation.

If you become enticed with the wisdom of science, the self-actualizing teachings of psychiatrists
or the excitement of fame and fortune, there is the
danger of losing contact with God and swearing that
you do not know Him--that there is no God.

Blasphemy against the Holy Ghost would be what
the Psalmist said: "The fool hath said in his heart,
there is no God!" (Psalms 17, and 53).

You can't be saved if you believe in your heart
that there is no Saviour--that there is no God.

Jesus has the power of God to save everyone who
calls upon Him, but He cannot save you against your
own will. No other person can save you. There is no
"power" which can save you--but once saved, there is
no outside power which can separate you from God.
140

IS THERE ONE TRUE CHURCH OF CHRIST?

"Upon this rock I will build My church."
Matthew 16:18

Yes! There is only one true Church of Christ.
No! There is no earthly true church of Christ.
Numerous paradoxes, dilemmas, parables, quandries, allegories, and metaphors, were used by Jesus to arouse people. Often when He told a parable the disciples came to Him later for an explanation.

Jesus did not want to be misunderstood, but He was aware that too direct a statement could anger religious leaders. Can you imagine the puzzled expressions when Jesus said that to save your life you must lose it?

We are in the same predicament when we contemplate whether we can point to one church and say that that is the only true church of Christ.

Christianity has been called a paradox. Who knows what a "paradox" is?

Gayle: "The dictionary says that a paradox is any statement which appears contradictory, unbelievable, or absurd, but may actually be true in fact. A paradox may also be self-contradictory, making the entire statement false. Jesus' statement, 'the last shall be first,' is a paradox. It is actually true, although it needs an explanation."

David reacts: "Then, what we're talking about can be put this way, 'There is only one Church, but there are many churches.' That seems confusing."

Paradoxes require clarifications. Failing to make the analogy intended with the paradox leads to false conclusions.

When Jesus replied to the "Good Confession" a new promise was given: He said, "Upon this rock I will build My church."

Two divergent doctrines have been formulated as to what Jesus meant.

<u>First</u>, because Jesus said to Peter he would henceforth be called Petros (rock), it has been claimed that upon Peter He would build His church. It is obvious that the first disciples considered

Peter to be a leader. When Paul was called back to
Jerusalem because he preached salvation to gentiles,
it was Peter who headed the judgmental apostles.
Paul taught salvation to non-Jews (gentiles), but
the apostles taught salvation only to Jews--Gentiles
had to become Jews before they could be Christians.

Second, the "Good Confession" Peter made was
declared to be the foundation upon which the church
of Christ would be built.

Salvation was to be based upon Jesus' statement, "Whosoever confesses Me before men, I will
confess before My Father which is in heaven." Only
Jewish people who accepted Jesus by that confession
were allowed to be members of the Jerusalem church.
The Jerusalem Christians thought of themselves as
being the only true church.

"Were either of these interpretations the correct interpretation of what Jesus was really talking
about?" asked Jesse. "We have such a multitude of
churches today that I can hardly believe any man-
made organization is what He was talking about."

"I don't know," Jennifer added. "I know there
are churches which claim to be the only true church.

"Some 'Jehovah's Witnesses' came to my door and
declared other churches were of the devil because
they were not following Jehovah's laws. To be acceptable to Jehovah, they said, I must join them."

We have been attempting to stay away from denominational and sectarian interpretations, but this
theme tonight entices us to see what different de-
nominations and other religions believe.

All vital religions in the world have dogmatic,
zealous, and even militant devotees proclaiming that
their's is the only true religion--that members of
that particular belief are the only true believers.

Can you imagine the quandary we would become
entangled with if we were to discuss the claims for
absolute truth in these various religions?

Remember the five blind men who touched the
elephant in different places? Each one could declare
their truth was the absolute truth because their experience proved what the elephant looked like. Had
they had been fanatics, they would have fought with
each other, not understanding that the elephant was
more than their single touch. None of them knew the
142

entire elephant, but each proclaimed the truth as he knew it to be.

The early disciples did not always agree. Paul and Barnabas worked together for several years. They evangelizing for Christ in Antioch so ardently that they were mockingly "Christians." A short time later they disagreed so violently that Barnabas departed for Crete with another companion, Mark. Paul took up with Silas (Acts 15:30). Most of Paul's letters were written to churches that were started with Silas.

Almost every letter Paul wrote contained pleas for unity of the spirit. Churches were divided by leaders who pretended to be the head of the church. Churches argued over who was most important; they split as they tried to determine who were eligible for baptism; they argued over who was authorized to teach in the church; who could partake of the Lord's Supper; who would eat first at their church dinners; and if idols were to be allowed in the church.

The book of Ephesians is an illustration of Paul's arguments for the unity of the church.

Laura, will you read Ephesians 4:3-6 for us?

Laura reads: "'I beseech you that you walk worthy of the vocation wherewith ye are called. Endeavoring to keep the unity of the Spirit in the bond of peace.

"There is one body, and one Spirit, even as ye are called in one hope of your calling; One Lord, one faith and one baptism. One God and Father of all, who is above all, and through all, and in you all.' That seems to be pretty clear and concise."

Do you get a better insight about the church Jesus was talking about? Do you think He was considering His statement that His kingdom is not of this world? Could it be that the Kingdom of God is synonymous with Jesus' statement of "My church," and "My Kingdom"? Also, how about this: "God is a Spirit and those who worship Him must worship in Spirit and in Truth" (John 4: 22).

Remember the statements we started with as to the one true church. The paradox is that both are true; they only refer to different things.

While Peter was certainly the central leader for Christians in Jerusalem, Paul was the one pleading for unity in the Spirit. Unity isn't by ecclesiastical bodies nor by creeds and doctrines, but in accepting that we are all one in Jesus Christ.

Our confession is not that Peter is the Christ; we do not call Paul our Saviour.

No matter what denomination our church may be, we should grant that others may have experienced God at different places and are proclaiming Jesus Christ with just a slightly different emphasis.

Humans have so many different needs that God may have shaped churches to those needs.

"My church emphasizes that we should have a basis for our belief. We are not told it is the only church of Christ, but that we are striving to live as close as possible to what we know of the Bible. I like the freedom that church gives me to explore the hidden meanings of Scriptures." Gayle commented.

Wouldn't it be a miracle if all churches could be that accepting of other churches? You must not forget Paul's admonition to test the spirits and see if they are loyal to Christ or if they're just using the church for selfish gains. Many times Paul warns about mixing with unbelievers (those who teach and believe in false doctrines). His statement in Second Corinthians 6:14 through 18 is outstandingly concise and frank. Here is the passage as paraphrased in The Living Bible:

"Don't be teamed with those who do not love the Lord, for what do the people of God have in common with people who sin? How can light live with darkness? What harmony can there be between Christ and the devil? How can a Christian be a partner with one who does not believe? And what union can there be between God's temple and idols? For you are God's temple, the home of the living God, and God has said of you, 'I will live in them and walk among them,and I will be their God and they shall be my people.' That is why The Lord has said, 'Leave them; separate yourselves from them; do not touch their filthy things, and I will welcome you, and be a Father to you, and you will be my sons and daughters.'"

Passages like these were directed at pagan practices and counterfeit religionists. They were not meant to separate bodies of believers.

The true church of Christ is spiritual, not structural.
144

WHAT IS HEAVEN?

"The Kingdom of Heaven is at hand."
Matthew 4:17

Heaven is mentioned 582 times in the Bible. It is a concept of every religion in the world. It has many different images or descriptions.

"I asked that question, because I heard one of Phil Donahue's talk shows a couple of years ago when he accused a Christian of being a bigot for stating that only those who accepted Jesus would enter into heaven. It made me wonder what a Christian meant by heaven, or what other religions might mean by their concepts of life after death," David explained.

Do you remember our first discussion about what heaven meant to most of the Old Testament writers?

Damon, "I was not here then. Would it be impolite to ask for a resume of that discussion?"

Let me introduce you to the group first. Damon is visiting a friend here and wanted to attend this meeting because he said his early religious training was so rigid that he rebelled and now calls himself an agnostic. He is going to college and majoring in psychology. As we talked, I became convinced he was not so much an agnostic as one who is searching for acceptable meanings to life's puzzles. He has been invited here to ask whatever questions are important to him.

Would one of you like to brief Damon on what we were talking about?

Jesse: "Let me try. We started with discussing the concept of the world in Biblical times, studying the days of creation and realizing how tiny and flat the world was thought to be. I was amazed with the solid 'firmament.' Then we looked up Scriptures and found that heaven was thought to be a solid residential area resting upon that solid sky. The limited scientific knowledge of the universe as well as the religious beliefs were not what I had thought. That limited knowledge remained at the time of Columbus.

"Also amazing was that the account of creation in Genesis follows the identical developments that modern scientists now depict in their theory of how the universe began. How could the writer of Genesis have written such a progression of creation prior to any biological, archeological, geological or astrological knowledge? How's that, Damon?"

"Actually," replied Damon, "I have thought that science and religion were conflicting disciplines. Religion is classified under philosophy. That puts science apart with its own pragmatic classification. Science deals with factual realities which can be measured, tested and reproduced. They have formulas and theories which can tested and proven to detect what is real and what is false.

"Religion has always been discussed as that which cannot have any scientific proof; therefore, it is myths and fantasies. I would be interested in how you claim religion can be proven."

Fair enough, but not in a way you might require it to be proven. Proof is not the same for science and religion.

As you said, scientists deal with physical data as measured by instruments they invented. They test what only what their equipment can handle, however.

They have no instrument for testing religion.

Religion is a phenomenon of the human spirit in relationship with God. It could be logical, mystic, earthly or heavenly. It is experienced by faith; it is practical or etherial, seen or unseen. And, it is all of these at once.

Again, we come to: <u>Christianity is a paradox</u>.

Religion deals with ultimate questions: "Who am I?" "Where did I come from?" "What is the meaning of life?" "What happens when I die?" "What is the purpose of the universe?" "Is there a God?"

Experience proves religion to individuals. The experiences can not be proven nor given to any other person. The receiving person has to internalize and "experience" the testimonies of other people, or the Bible, in order to have an experience of faith.

John Paul Sartre, the French "Existentialist," had his whole philosophy based on this principle: if you can accept that something exists, it does exist for you. If you can accept there is a God, then He
146

exists to you; if you cannot accept a belief in God, God does not exist, to you. He said that nothing is real unless you experience it as existing.

Enough diversion. Back to discussing heaven.

Several years ago I attended a discourse about heaven. The lecturer was a gray-haired and stately theologian who was old enough to have been in heaven already. The question time after his lecture asked him to describe heaven.

The lecturer went into deep reflection, smiled quietly, then replied, "I am sorry, but I just can't quite remember."

There is no way we could give an adequate presentation of heaven. Jesus didn't attempt to picture heaven, rather, He used illustrations which pointed to heavenly attributes. Here are some of the many illustrations Jesus used, as recorded in The Living Bible:

"The Kingdom of Heaven is like a farmer sowing good seeds in his field, an enemy came at night and sowed weeds. He advised his workers to let both grow and that the weeds would be burned at the time of harvest" (Matthew 13:24-29).

"The Kingdom of Heaven is like a mustard seed (a very tiny seed) which grows to become one of the largest trees so that birds can find shelter therein" (Matthew 13:29-32).

"The Kingdom of Heaven is like a woman baking bread, she uses yeast which permeates every part" (Matthew 13:33).

"The Kingdom of Heaven is like a treasure which a man finds in a field, sells everything else he has in order to buy the field and possess the treasure" (Matthew 13:44).

"The Kingdom of Heaven is like a pearl merchant who found a pearl of great value. He sold everything he had in order to buy the pearl of great price" (Matthew 13:45,46).

"The Kingdom of Heaven is like a fisherman who makes a great catch, takes them to the beach to sort out and toss away the fish unfit to eat" (Matthew 13:47,48).

Jesus said that would be the way it would be at the end of the world; those who were righteous would be separated from those who were bad: those who were evil would burn in the fire of hell where they would weep and gnash their teeth, but the righteous would receive everlasting life in heaven (Matt.13:37-42).

He also gave the illustration that the Kingdom of Heaven is like a king who balanced his books and found a man who owed him a lot of money. He called the man before him and demanded full payment. when the man pled for forgiveness, he was forgiven, then went out and demanded repayment of a debt owed him. That debtor could not pay, so the forgiven man threw his debtor thrown into prison. The king heard about it and became very angry. He called back the man he had forgiven and reprimanded him, saying that in the manner he was forgiven he should also have forgiven his debtor. The king then had the debtor put into a torture chamber until he could pay his entire debt (Matthew 18: 20-35).

Another illustration was of a farmer who hired harvesters at different times of the day, paying the same wage to all. The first laborers complained because, they argued, they had worked longer so should have received more, but the paymaster reminded them that they all received what they had agreed to work for. No wrong was done to them (Matthew 20:1-15).

Look at the illustration in Matthew 22:1-14 of the wedding feast where the invited guests failed to show up. He told his servants to run throughout the city and invite everyone. One man showed up without the proper attire, so was thrown out into the outer darkness. Jesus' message was: "Many are called, but few are chosen."

Also, Matthew 25:1-14 tells of bridesmaids who were to carry lamps to light the way to the wedding. Five kept their lights ready, but five let the lamps die out. When the bridegroom came and needed lamps to light his way, there was not time to go get fuel for the useless lamps, so they were locked out from the wedding feast. He gave this illustration to make a point: be always ready because you do not know the date or hour when The Lord will return.

"Then where do we get such precise pictures of heaven?" Jennifer asked. "If Jesus did not give the exact nature of heaven, are our images of heaven all just man-made? I have been excited most of my life to get into the glory of heaven as described to me."

148

Without entering a controversy over meanings of the entire book of Revelations, let us turn to that book to answer Jennifer's questions. We do not know who "John," the author, actually was. Some Bible researchers think he was John the beloved, the youngest of the disciples. It may be that in his old age, after seeing the other disciples die, he was meditating about eternity and received a beatific dream.

"What's 'beatific'? You use words I do not understand." Jesse protested.

Gayle, "That means blissful or blessed. It may mean happiness, delightful or joyful as well. That's the kind of experience I had a few years ago. I wish I could have that kind of experience again."

Whatever else may be read into Revelations, the visions of John certainly was intended to encourage and give spiritual strength to the churches Paul had helped establish in Asia Minor. They needed John's assurance: even though they might die as martyrs, a glorious reward would be their's in heaven.

John's heaven tells of gates as having 12 great pearls; a city built with gold; magnificent mansions and God sitting on His throne with saints and angels of heaven encircled Him singing His praises. Also in heaven was the Tree of Life from the Garden of Eden.

Heaven's foundations were made with 12 precious gems; there was no night there; there was no need of sun or moon. Everyone would wear the starry crown of righteousness.

Harps, stars in my crown, a half-way place such as purgatory, separation of family units, different sized houses, differing levels of honor and recognition, masters and servant--all are pictures from the excited imaginations of mankind. If these concepts help to identify the glories of eternity, use them. Just do not forget that heaven is greater than your greatest imagined glory.

Personally, I see heaven being a spiritual existence. I do not know what I will experience when I get into heaven. I have alluded to many things when counseling about death and in funeral messages such as: "into the arms of God," "crossing the bar," "a place prepared for you," "sailing to another land," "beyond the sunset," and "meeting loved ones." None of these are exactly correct, nor are they false.

"What do other religions believe about heaven?"
Laura wanted to know.

The group answered Laura and discussed religion
of many peoples, and compiled a list of beliefs:

1. Confucianism believes in a family relationship which goes between life on earth and eternity.
Aged persons are to be honored for wisdom and closeness to their ancestors.

Confucius taught that there are ten rounds of
existence, each wiser than before, but determined
at birth to have the characteristics of that year.

Earthly rounds of existences end with forever
living in the family of heavenly ancestors.

2. Moslems envision eternal life as living in a
beautiful, cool valley with trees and grasses and a
stream of clear water. It is a man's realm. A woman
may be there as a man's attendant, but she can not
achieve it on her own merit.

3. American Indians have many images of heaven,
but generally hold that it is a happy hunting ground
with many animals and fish. Funeral rites included
foods, hunting equipment, trinkets and other living
necessities. The place of the dead was holy ground,
and was inhabited by ancestral spirits. Folk-tales
and Myths tell of departed spirits returning in the
bodies of animals, birds or people to bless or curse
friend or foe. Their affinity with nature was close
to ancient animism, but they believed in more individual honors and the affinity with nature.

4. Mayas, Incas, Aztecs and Toltecs, the major
groups of Mexican and South American indians, held
differing views of life after death, but most were
vague concepts of unity with a heavenly life-force.
Mayans believed that life emerged from a snake which
came up from the ground and breathed out human life.
Their ball game ended in the captain of the winning
team being honored as one who deserved to enter into
the presence of that life-force, so his head was cut
off to liberate his spirit. The mural carved in the
stone wall of the ball court shows the spirit of the
captain ascending from his body like snakes. Eagles
and jaguars were also considered sacred.

5. Jehovah's Witnesses had visited with some in
the group who were told that Jehovah's Witnesses believe in a future here on earth. Earth, to them, is
150

to become renewed; it will be inhabited by Witnesses who will be the governing 144,000 chosen ones. Common citizens will work under these rulers. No other "Christian" will be allowed in this heaven.

6. The Worldwide Church of God teaches almost an identical heavenly concept as the Jehovah's Witnesses. Membership in that organization is required in order to have a place in their heaven.

7. The Old Testament is involved more with the everlasting covenant God made with Abraham and the Jewish nation than with any grand image of eternity. While they thought of God as inhabiting the residential place attached just above the firmament there, is very little discussion about humans getting into that place. The first Psalm depicts rewards of the Godly and the ungodly, but emphasizes how a person is to live; it ends by a warning about the Judgment Day but merely says that the unrighteous are doomed.

Jacob's dream of a ladder ascending to heaven depicts angels of heaven upon the ladder, but he was not invited to climb the ladder into heaven.

Some prophets were "caught up in the air"; some "went to be with their fathers." We recognize that Jewish theologians could cut these explanations into pieces. Judaism is much more intricate than we have expressed.

8. Christians have so much disagreement that it is impossible to formulate a finite picture. Heaven is said to be: (a) on earth; (b) on some distant star; (c) a physical place somewhere over the earth, but what part of the round earth is heaven "above"? (d) a spiritual existence with God.

Some believe heaven will not receive humans before the end of the world, but there are others who believe that those who accept Jesus Christ will rise with Him into paradise immediately when they die.

Thanks for joining in the discussions tonight, Damon. I hope some of your questions were answered. One thing you might carry out of this session is the understanding that throughout the religions efforts to picture heaven come from sincere convictions that heaven is something glorious, something beyond Man's greatest dreams.

Damon: "I can't say that I agree with what you have said, but I will have to admit that this group has made me think about the reality of things I have been denying. Will it be possible for you to record what you have been saying so I can study some of the arguments?"

We have been thinking about that, Damon. There are many problems to that, but with your help, and a lot of patience, it might be accomplished.

While we have been adventuring into the nature of God, we have said many times that we do not have the only insights. What insights we have are indicators that there is much, much more to God than can ever be comprehended by Man.

It would be repetitious to list the attributes of God. While redundancy is a normal practice with teachers and counselors as a method of implanting a lesson, it would not be profitable for us.

Redundancy would be if we said, "God is love," then repeat by saying that God loves us.

The problem is that none of us agree exactly in the definition of "love." And that means that none of us can agree exactly about what God is.

You are the only one who can overcome the doubt in your heart. God offers His love, but you must be the one who accepts it. We can share with you what we have experienced with God, but you are the one to accept or reject those experiences in order for you for you to know God is with you and that heaven is a reality.

You are invited to be with us next time when we discuss eternal life.

WILL I HAVE ETERNAL LIFE?

"The gift of God is eternal life through Jesus Christ the Lord."
Romans 6:23

What have you found out about an eternal life? You are free to recall past discussions which help you clarify your answers.

David, "I've looked up a lot of references with my computer, but I still have my questions. Why are we so driven to believe that we will have an eternal life? As far as can be determined, no other animal has life after death. Why should we think we are so different from other animals?"

Your scientific mode of thinking may be showing through. Humans are scientifically classified to be animals, aren't they? We believe that when animals die, their total life ends. They have no soul. They have no heaven to gain nor hell to shun. People who do not believe in God would have us believe that we are like any other animal.

"It seems to me, then, that we've been discussing two things," Jesse offered. "First, the reality of having a 'soul'; and second, what is the expectation for our souls when we die? I have been having many new thoughts during these discussions, and this past week opened up an expanded understanding of the Bible. I didn't know that the entire Bible was written with the assumption that everyone had a soul."

Laura: "I have deep feelings that I would like my beloved dog to be with me in heaven. I know that we have been saying only humans have souls, but I'd expect most pet owners would prefer to believe that their pets could be in heaven with them."

There is no doubt about that. However, tonight our discussion is about the meanings and wonders of eternal life for you.

Historical data of experiences with ghosts, appearances of persons from the past, the teachings of reincarnation, seances, precognition and the universal quest for understanding about what happens to us when we die, all lead us to this conclusion: there's "something" within us more than just an animal body.

Gayle: "That brings up the thought I have been having this week. I began reading the book of Genesis, but didn't get beyond those first two chapters. They tell two stories of the creation of mankind.

"The first is the story of Adam and Eve created in the likeness of God, but doesn't distinguish the body from the soul," Gayle continued. "Chapter two tells of forming a body out of clay, telling us of the physical formation of Man from the dust of the earth. It doesn't say the body was formed after the likeness of God. I deduced from these passages that God made a body first, then breathed His breath into that body and Man became a living soul. How can we put these two passages together?"

You have been thinking about those passages all week. Why not share with us whatever you got out of them?

"Really, I have been in a quandary. I've had so much of the pros and cons on the abortion issue that the dilemma of when human existence starts has me in a quandary. My early religious education taught that God was a physical being, that He resembled an aged, robust man with a long, gray beard sitting upon His golden throne. The account in chapter one fits perfectly into that type of a God who created Man in His own physical image. You see, I came here with more questions than answers," Gayle replied.

I could confuse you even more with the question of what actually is Man then? Is Man physical? Sure! Man is not just a shadow upon earth's stage as some Greek philosophers proposed, nor some kind of mere "thought," as some religious bodies believe. Man is from the dust of the earth, solid and actual. Physical formation is the emphasis of the story in Genesis 2:7. That passage appears to differ from the creation story of Genesis 1:26,27.

Genesis 2:7 gives an additional emphasis. Man did not become a "living soul' until after the body was completed; until the body had reached the capability to be a living soul.

What is God? That's right: God is a spirit.

"I thought we had been talking about God as the only Spirit," Jennifer mused. "You said 'a' spirit.
154

Shouldn't you have just said that God is spirit and just another of many spirits?"

You have a good ear, Jennifer. You are correct. God is ONE. The way I used the word indicated something opposite from physical, so I said "a" spirit.

Does this say something about the relationship between Man's image and God?

That brings up another question, what would be the value of making males and females as only physical bodies when the image of God is spirit? Is this possible: Genesis 1:26,27 is the same story as 2:7? There may have been differing interpretations about Genesis 1:27 when it was first written, and required specific clarification of its meaning as told in the second chapter.

What about the statement we made before: "Your concept of heaven determines your concept of God and Man"? Yes, you could put it an other way, your idea of God determines your concept of heaven and of Man. Do not make your God so small that you can hold Him within the confines of your own mind.

If "I" am something inhabiting this body, then what happens to "me" when death comes?

The story of the Garden of Eden tells that God did not want Man's body to live forever. To prevent Adam and Eve from eating of the Tree of Life, which would give their bodies eternity, God expelled them from the garden.

Here I become facetious again, but only to draw attention to what I have found to be the truth. How often have you heard, or read, that God created the world in six days, then rested? That is the justification for keeping the seventh day as the Sabbath, a day of rest. The Israelites could work six days, but had to keep the seventh a holy day for rest and worship. Facetiously, I wondered that if God has been sitting on His throne and resting ever since the end of the sixth day, who was busy guiding the children of Israel with Moses, teaching the prophets, answering prayers and begetting His only begotten Son?

God so loves the world that He never rests. He works so Man can choose to receive eternal life.

My nature makes me answer my own facetiousness. I think John 1:1-3 gives some clarification when it states that in the beginning all things were <u>made</u> by

Him. God did <u>physical</u> creating during the first six
days, the first six epochs of time. God made everything that needed to be made. When He finished His
work, He made the observation that it was very good.

John writes that God continues spiritual work.
He became flesh. He was active. Mankind met Him.

The history of Job emphasizes that God is where
we are--we cannot escape from His presence. David,
the Psalmists, wrote: "He that keepeth Israel shall
neither slumber nor sleep" (Psalms 121:4).

I cannot agree with John Calvin that God made
the world, set it in motion, predetermined all which
was to be, then went somewhere and is "resting."

God cares and is knowledgeable about our lives,
but doesn't manipulate us because He has given to us
freedom to live righteous lives, which includes the
freedom to live evil lives. We must choose our own
way of life. It isn't so much how we live our lives,
but how we relate to Jesus Christ which determines
what happens when we die. Paul wrote: "The wages of
sin is death, but the gift of God is eternal life
through Jesus Christ, the Lord" (Romans 6: 23).

The New Testament is full of declarations that
you will have eternal life. We have another quandary
here. We discussed the meaning of "eternity" as it
related to God, but what does it mean as it relates
to us?

Laura, "I want to play forever with my dog when
I get to heaven. I also expect to enjoy friendships
and family."

Jesse, "A good job and a loving family would be
my choice for eternity."

"Not me, I want to see all the mysteries of the
universe," David said. "The universe is so huge I'll
probably need an eternity to get through it all. I'd
want to find out how there can be an infinite expansion to the universe--and what there is beyond that
infinity. An expanding universe implies an expansion
into something, but into what? Does there exist an
infinite expansion of nothingness where the universe
goes? What are the boundaries of infinity?"

This is a good time to bring up your thought of
a fourth dimension.

You also made me consider the reality of there
being a fifth dimension.

The more I thought about it, the more it became
logical, except it took on another meaning. A fourth
dimension actually fits into a religious concept of
the universe. A fifth dimension is also a religious
concept, although not identified as such. When theo-
logions and astrophysicists conjecture about the un-
knowns they may find interest in these definitions:

ETERNITY: the fourth dimension.(Timelessness)

INFINITY: the fifth dimension. (Endlessness)

With infinity, the universe can expand forever.
It is the same concept as how many angels will stand
on the point of a needle. A finite universe always
needs to be defined--boundaries must be drawn. That
does not relate to infinity which is always an unexplainable limitlessness.

With eternity considered, the birth or termination of the universe become meaningless, just as the
ancient Hindu explanation showed the reincarnations
of universe after universe without end. Prognostic
religious thought may be the linkage modern science
is looking for to explain what it has discovered as
mysteries.

Gayle: "I work hard with school students. I'd
like to think of eternal life as existing forever in
an atmosphere of loving peace."

Jesse had a hard time expressing himself: "If
eternity is a condition without time, why do I think
of heaven as a place where there is on-going action?
I accept that my soul came from God, but I wonder if
death releases my soul to return to God and I become
merge with God? Do I return into God's everlasting
spirit? Would I be an identity in eternity?"

"I can't understand that," Jennifer protested.
"I want to be myself in eternity. I expect Jesus to
meet me face to face. I want to see Him smile at me
and take me into His loving arms."

Frankl's book talks about God living in our unconsciousness and emerging into our awareness as our
conscience. Jung talked of a universal urge to perfection working through all of us. Jesus gave this
promise: "Verily, verily I say unto you, he that
believeth on me hath eternal life" (John 6:47).

The LIVING BIBLE states it this way: "How earnestly I tell you this: anyone who believes in me already has eternal life."

You are living in eternity right now. Is that shocking? If you can accept that the eternal God is with you, why not recognize that you are already experiencing something of eternity?

Jesse's question may be answered with an illustration. Suppose an individual is as a drop of rain. Billions of drops could exist. Where would they all come from? They come from earth's vast body of water which is actually one cohesive unity. Where do drops of rain go? Back into that one body.

Suppose each drop has an intelligence--a soul. When it drops back into the ocean, does it become an ocean? Or, does it merge into the essence of the universal body? Will it have infinite awareness of all the other drops of water which also merged into the infinity of eternal oneness?

Do not be upset with that. Some day we will know. It does not affect how we should live today.

No ultimate answer can be given. Let your own experiences will guide you. Let your questing open to the infinite love and power of God. You can know God in part, but that can not change His reality.

Never get caught in the complacency of thinking that you know everything, nor in the depression that you can never know the ultimate truths.

We have not formulated easy or dogmatic answers for you. Your own experiences and logic should help you find your purpose for living, as well as giving you the assurance that your future life will be full and an unimaginatively grand experience.

You have also experienced that your life can be enriched by sharing insights with other people.

May your journey of faith forever be exciting; may you comprehend the many variations among persons and be accepting of them.

May your life be as abundant, fruitful, confident and full of joy as Jesus can enable it to be.

Live without fear, for God is love and He is abiding with you.

EXPERIENCING GOD
IS TO LIVE WITHOUT FEAR.

INDEX

SOURCE MATERIALS

BERRY, Gerald L. <u>Religions of the World (From Prim
itive Times to the 20th Century)</u>. Barnes &
Noble, Inc., New York, 1947.

ERDOES, Richard, Alfonso Ortiz, ed. <u>American Indian
Myths and Legends.</u> Pantheon Books, N. Y., 1984.

FRANKL, Viktor E. <u>Man's Search For Meaning</u>. Pocket
Books, New York, N.Y. 1959

<u>Great Religions of the World</u>, National Geographic
Society, 1978

HAMILTON, Edith, <u>Mythology</u>. Little, Brown and Com
pany, Boston, Mass. 1942

HAWKING, Stephen, <u>A Brief History Of Time</u>. Bantam
Books, New York, N.Y. 1988

JENKINS, David E. <u>The Glory Of Man</u>. Charles Scrib-
ner's Sons, New York, N.Y. 1969

<u>Jesus And His Times</u>, The Reader's Digest Associa-
tion, July, 1990

LaHAYE, Tim, <u>The Battle For The Mind</u>. Fleming H.
Revel Company, Old Tappan, New Jersey, 1980

<u>LIFE</u>, December, 1990, Life-Time Publishing Company

KALAKAUA, King David, <u>The Legends And Myths Of
Hawaii</u> Charles Tuttle Company, Rutland, Ver-
mont, 1972

<u>OMNI</u>, February, 1990, Omni Publications Inter-
national, New York, N.Y.

PARRINDER, Geoffrey, ed. <u>World Religions,</u> From Ancient History to the Present. Facts On File
Publications, New York, 1971.

PECK, Dr. M. Scott, <u>People Of The Lie</u>. Simon and
Schuster, Inc. New York, N.Y. 1983

PRABHUPADA, A.C.Bhaktivedanta Swami. <u>Srimad Bhagava-
tam</u>. The Bhaktivedanta Book Trust, Los Angeles,
California. 1976

PELIKAN, Jaroslav, ed. <u>The World Treasury of Modern
Religious Thought</u>. Little, Brown and Company,
Boston, Mass. 1990

STENSON, Sten H. <u>Sense and Nonsense In Religion</u>, An
Essay on the Language and Phenomenology of
Religion, Abingdon Press, N.Y. 1969

Watchtower Tract Society, <u>Man's Search for God</u>, 1990